David J. Ludwig, PhD, MDiv
Editor

Social Work
and the Family Unit

Social Work and the Family Unit has been co-published
simultaneously as *Journal of Family Social Work*,
Volume 4, Number 3 2000.

Pre-Publication
REVIEWS,
COMMENTARIES,
EVALUATIONS . . .

"**A**t a time when the family unit
is under severe attack and
when parents are asking for help
in regaining control of their families, this book is a must read. A
must read for social workers and
counselors whose goal is to
strengthen and enhance both the
spiritual and emotional components of family relationships by focusing on what brought the family
together in the beginning–the desire to form a unit called 'WE.'"

Col. Jim Schlie
Executive Director
for Family Connection
Lutheran Family Association
St. Louis, MO

"This book goes a long way in terms of integrating the disciplines of family therapy, psychotherapy and spiritual care to provide relational systems tools for those working with contemporary families. David Ludwig has included a number of contributors who are practitioners in these areas and have collaborated in the development of this emerging model.

In the first part of the book you will find a practical, holistic approach that can help various types of families move away from existing blame cycles and begin to discover more functional ways of relating as families.

If you want to know how narrative and other therapists relate to pastoral care, etc., Donald Bardill's chapter is most helpful. The concluding chapter is based on a study of the relationship between spirituality and life experience, examines its implications for practitioners and suggests areas for further research.

It is entirely appropriate that we enter the new millennium with a groundbreaking publication that challenges the 20th century divide between secular therapy and spiritual care."

Karl Brettig, BA
Program Director
Para Vista Luthern Church
South Australia

"The Ludwig and Knippa articles present language along with strategies that can be used in conveying the importance of the 'WE' in relationships. Murphy offers practical approaches in helping families see the 'WE' in their family. Opper does the same with the step-family. Just as the essential 'WE' is often invisible to clients in relationships, so is the spirit of the relationship as Ludwig and Bardill point out. This series of articles will be especially helpful to the new therapist because it offers a way to give voice to these unseen dimensions.

The practiced therapist will find the language refreshing and as a result may add new words to their practice vocabulary. The strategies are helpful because they offer ways of challenging clients. And whether a new or practiced therapist, the theory of Bardill's article and the research on the religious/spiritual dimension in counseling of Joanides et al. affirms the work of integrating one's secular training with one's belief in a Christian world view. The book succeeds in offering ideas and ways to present the essential 'WE' and the importance of the spiritual in individual and relationship development."

Barbara Brunworth, PhD
President
Lutheran Counseling Services, Inc.
Dallas/Ft. Worth, TX

Social Work
and the Family Unit

Social Work and the Family Unit has been co-published simultaneously as *Journal of Family Social Work*, Volume 4, Number 3 2000.

The *Journal of Family Social Work* Monographic "Separates"

(formerly the *Journal of Social Work & Human Sexuality* series)*

For information on previous issues of the *Journal of Social Work & Human Sexuality* series, please contact: The Haworth Press, Inc., 10 Alice Street, Binghamton, NY 13904-1580 USA.

Below is a list of "separates," which in serials librarianship means a special issue simultaneously published as a special journal issue or double-issue *and* as a "separate" hardbound monograph. (This is a format which we also call a "DocuSerial.")

"Separates" are published because specialized libraries or professionals may wish to purchase a specific thematic issue by itself in a format which can be separately cataloged and shelved, as opposed to purchasing the journal on an on-going basis. Faculty members may also more easily consider a "separate" for classroom adoption.

"Separates" are carefully classified separately with the major book jobbers so that the journal tie-in can be noted on new book order slips to avoid duplicate purchasing.

You may wish to visit Haworth's website at . . .

http://www.haworthpressinc.com

. . . to search our online catalog for complete tables of contents of these separates and related publications.

You may also call 1-800-HAWORTH (outside US/Canada: 607-722-5857), or Fax 1-800-895-0582 (outside US/Canada: 607-771-0012), or e-mail at:

getinfo@haworthpressinc.com

Social Work and the Family Unit, edited by David J. Ludwig, PhD, MDiv (Vol. 4, No. 3, 2000). *Offers therapists methods and suggestions for helping clients focus on problems within relationships and provides techniques and examples for conducting more successful and productive sessions.*

The Family, Spirituality, and Social Work, edited by Dorothy S. Becvar, MSW, PhD (Vol. 2, No. 4, 1998). *"This groundbreaking text is an evocative excursion into the realm of 'spirituality' within the domain of human services and treatment." (Marcia D. Brown-Standridge, ACSW, PhD, private practice, Terre Haute, Indiana)*

Cross-Cultural Practice with Couples and Families, edited by Philip M. Brown, PhD, LCSW, and John S. Shalett, MSW, BCSW (Vol. 2, No. 1/2, 1997). *"An excellent resource for practitioners and educators alike. It is an eye-opener and a first step in the process of understanding true diversity and cultural sensitivity." (Multicultural Review)*

Sexuality and Disabilities: A Guide for Human Service Practitioners, edited by Romel W. Mackelprang, DSW, MSW, and Deborah Valentine, PhD, MSW (Vol. 8, No. 2, 1993).* *"Emphasizes the need for individualized counseling in a supportive, educational context." (Science Books and Films)*

Adolescent Sexuality: New Challenges for Social Work, edited by Paula Allen-Meares, PhD, MSW, and Constance Hoenk Shapiro, PhD, MSW (Vol. 8, No. 1, 1989).* *"This is a valuable and wide-ranging look at the vital, complex, and very specific issues of adolescent sexuality and their implications for social work and social workers." (Paul H. Ephross, PhD, Professor, School of Social Work and Community Planning, University of Maryland at Baltimore)*

Treatment of Sex Offenders in Social Work and Mental Health Settings, edited by John S. Wodarski, PhD, and Daniel Whitaker, MSW (Vol. 7, No. 2, 1989).* *"The editors, besides contributing their own share of expertise, surrounded themselves with scientific experts who clearly enunciated their experiences in research design, data, conclusions, and applications." (Journal of the American Association of Psychiatric Administrators)*

The Sexually Unusual: Guide to Understanding and Helping, edited by Dennis M. Dailey, DSW (Vol. 7, No. 1, 1989).* *"If you want to know what you don't know about human sexual behavior, I challenge you to read this book, which is timely, cogent, and without a doubt, superior to any other book on this subject." (Arthur Herman, MSW, Chief Social Worker and Associate Director, Center for Sexual Health, Menninger Clinic, The Menninger Foundation, Topeka, Kansas)*

Sociological Aspects of Sexually Transmitted Diseases, edited by Margaret Rodway and Marianne Wright (Vol. 6, No. 2, 1988).* *"The most comprehensive resource guide on the topic of sexually transmitted diseases. It belongs in all the libraries of helping professionals and students, and is an up-to-date volume on an emerging issue in the field of human sexuality." (Professor Benjamin Schlesinger, Faculty of Social Work, University of Toronto, Canada; Author of Sexual Behavior in Canada (University of Toronto Press))*

Infertility and Adoption: A Guide for Social Work Practice, edited by Deborah Valentine (Vol. 6, No. 1, 1988).* *"Provides educators and practitioners with a rich compendium of information that will not only enhance their understanding of the dynamics involved in assessing and treating individuals and families presenting with concerns around fertility and adoption, but also provide an expanded context that takes into consideration program and policy issues." (Sadye L. Logan, DSW, Associate Professor, University of Kansas, School of Social Welfare)*

Intimate Relationships: Some Social Work Perspectives on Love, edited by Wendell Ricketts, BA, and Harvey Gochros, PhD (Vol. 5, No. 2, 1987).* *Insightful perspectives on the social worker's role in the counseling of clients who have problems with different kinds of love.*

Adolescent Sexualities: Overviews and Principles of Intervention, edited by Paula Allen-Meares, PhD, and David A. Shore, PhD (Vol. 5, No. 1, 1986).* *"The collection moves beyond many other articles and books by offering practical solutions and ideas for individuals working with adolescents." (SIECUS Report)*

Human Sexuality, Ethnoculture, and Social Work, edited by Larry Lister, DSW (Vol. 4, No. 3, 1987).* *A valuable work providing basic cultural information within the context of human sexuality of several ethnocultural groups.*

Social Work Practice in Sexual Problems, edited by James Gripton, DSW, and Mary Valentich, PhD (Vol. 4, No. 1/2, 1986).* *"Serves as a valuable resource since it appears to encompass the major areas related to sexual problems." (Shankar A. Yelaja, DSW, Dean, Faculty of Social Work, Wilfrid Laurier University)*

Feminist Perspectives on Social Work and Human Sexuality, edited by Mary Valentich, PhD, and James Gripton, PhD, DSW (Vol. 3, No. 2/3, 1985).* *"Contains a powerful and unnerving message for educators, clinicians, and students. . . . important and useful . . . a valued addition to professional as well as academic libraries." (Canadian Social Work Review)*

Homosexuality and Social Work, edited by Robert Schoenberg, ACSW, and Richard S. Goldberg, MSS (Vol. 2, No. 2/3, 1984).* *"Packed with useful information on the special problems of both gay and lesbian clients. . . . A treasured resource for nurses, counselors, physicians, and other helping professionals." (Contemporary Sociology)*

Human Sexuality in Medical Social Work, edited by Larry Lister, DSW, and David A. Shore, PhD (Vol. 2, No. 1, 1984).* *"Excellently researched and written. . . . The role of the social worker as a member of the health care team is very well highlighted. . . . makes a valuable contribution to the counseling community." (Journal of Sex Education & Therapy)*

Social Work and Child Sexual Abuse, edited by Jon R. Conte, PhD, and David A. Shore, PhD (Vol. 1, No. 1/2, 1982).* *"This volume is a solid one, which contains a wealth of knowledge for the helping professional." (The Canadian Journal of Human Sexuality)*

Social Work and the Family Unit

David J. Ludwig, PhD, MDiv
Editor

Social Work and the Family Unit has been co-published
simultaneously as *Journal of Family Social Work,*
Volume 4, Number 3 2000.

The Haworth Press, Inc.
New York • London • Oxford

Social Work and the Family Unit has been co-published simultaneously as *Journal of Family Social Work,* Volume 4, Number 3 2000.

The Haworth Press, Inc., 10 Alice Street, Binghamton, NY 13904-1580 USA

Cover design by Thomas J. Mayshock Jr.

Library of Congress Cataloging-in-Publication Data

Social work and the family unit / David J. Ludwig, editor.
    p. cm.
    "Co-published simultaneously as Journal of family social work, volume 4, number 3, 2000."
    Includes bibliographical references and index.
    ISBN 0-7890-1196-4 (alk. paper) – ISBN 0-7890-1197-2 (alk. paper)
    1. Communication in the family. 2. Interpersonal communication. 3. Family psychotherapy.
4. Family–Religious life. I. Ludwig, David J. II. Journal of family social work, v. 4, no. 3.
HQ518 .S64 2000
362.82'86–dc21
                                                                              00-040845

INDEXING & ABSTRACTING

Contributions to this publication are selectively indexed or abstracted in print, electronic, online, or CD-ROM version(s) of the reference tools and information services listed below. This list is current as of the copyright date of this publication. See the end of this section for additional notes.

- *Abstracts in Anthropology*
- *Abstracts in Social Gerontology: Current Literature on Aging*
- *Abstracts of Research in Pastoral Care & Counseling*
- *Applied Social Sciences Index & Abstracts (ASSIA) (Online: ASSI via Data-Star) (CDRom: ASSIA Plus)*
- *BUBL Information Service: An Internet-based Information Service for the UK higher education community <URL: http://bubl.ac.uk/>*
- *Cambridge Scientific Abstracts (Health & Safety Science Abstracts/Risk Abstracts)*
- *caredata CD: the social & community care database*
- *Child Development Abstracts & Bibliography*
- *CINAHL (Cumulative Index to Nursing & Allied Health Literature), in print, also on CD-ROM from CD PLUS, EBSCO, and SilverPlatter, and online from CDP Online (formerly BRS), Data-Star, and PaperChase*
- *CNPIEC Reference Guide: Chinese National Directory of Foreign Periodicals*
- *Criminal Justice Abstracts*
- *Digest of Neurology and Psychiatry*
- *Educational Administration Abstracts (EAA)*
- *ERIC Clearinghouse on Counseling and Student Services (ERIC/CASS)*
- *Family Studies Database (online and CD/ROM)*
- *Family Violence & Sexual Assault Bulletin*
- *FINDEX <www.publist.com>*
- *Human Resources Abstracts (HRA)*
- *IBZ International Bibliography of Periodical Literature*
- *Index to Periodical Articles Related to Law*
- *Linguistics and Language Behavior Abstracts (LLBA) <www.csa.com>*
- *Mental Health Abstracts (online through DIALOG)*

(continued)

- *National Criminal Justice Reference Service*
- *PASCAL, c/o Institute de L'Information Scientifique et Technique*
- *Periodica Islamica*
- *Psychological Abstracts (PsycINFO)*
- *Referativnyi Zhurnal (Abstracts Journal of the All-Russian Institute of Scientific and Technical Information)*
- *Sage Family Studies Abstracts (SFSA)*
- *Social Services Abstracts <www.csa.com>*
- *Social Work Abstracts*
- *Sociological Abstracts (SA) <www.csa.com>*
- *Studies on Women Abstracts*
- *Violence and Abuse Abstracts: A Review of Current Literature on Interpersonal Violence (VAA)*

Special Bibliographic Notes related to special journal issues (separates) and indexing/abstracting:

- indexing/abstracting services in this list will also cover material in any "separate" that is co-published simultaneously with Haworth's special thematic journal issue or DocuSerial. Indexing/abstracting usually covers material at the article/chapter level.
- monographic co-editions are intended for either non-subscribers or libraries which intend to purchase a second copy for their circulating collections.
- monographic co-editions are reported to all jobbers/wholesalers/approval plans. The source journal is listed as the "series" to assist the prevention of duplicate purchasing in the same manner utilized for books-in-series.
- to facilitate user/access services all indexing/abstracting services are encouraged to utilize the co-indexing entry note indicated at the bottom of the first page of each article/chapter/contribution.
- this is intended to assist a library user of any reference tool (whether print, electronic, online, or CD-ROM) to locate the monographic version if the library has purchased this version but not a subscription to the source journal.
- individual articles/chapters in any Haworth publication are also available through the Haworth Document Delivery Service (HDDS).

Social Work and the Family Unit

CONTENTS

ABOUT THE EDITOR

David J. Ludwig, PhD, MDiv, is Chair of the Psychology and Sociology Department at Lenoir-Rhyne College, Hickory, North Carolina, where he teaches courses in the personality and clinical areas. He received his PhD in experimental psychology from Washington University in 1966. He is also a graduate of Concordia Seminary, St. Louis, and is an ordained Lutheran minister and assistant to the pastor at Christ Lutheran Church in Hickory. Dr. Ludwig maintains a private practice as a licensed therapist. He has written 6 books and 3 video series in addition to over 100 articles in popular and professional journals. He conducts seminars on the relationship of faith to personal and family life, most recently returning from in-depth training of church professionals in Australia.

Preface

This book focuses on the overwhelming importance of relationships in working with the individual and with families. The clear emphasis of this volume on the family unit as a real entity is an emphatic statement that the client(s) usually focus on the wrong thing as the problem. Usually there is blame, accompanied with the statement, "If only . . . ," when assessing the problem. If the counselor affirms this perception, the client(s) are robbed of their power to change the situation.

It is not only more accurate to focus on the relationship as the problem, but this focus also empowers the clients. The lead article, "It's the Relationship, Stupid!" gives specific case descriptions of this insight. When dealing with a problem teenager, both parents blame the other and want the other to change. When the couple focused on their relationship as the basis of the problem, then each had the power to do something with their half of the relationship. They found that when they formed a united front, the situation changed. The lead article also focuses on the internal distress of the individual who usually blames another person and the situation for the distress. Again, it is more accurate and empowering to see it as a problem with the person's relationship with self.

The second article by Alex Opper is titled "What Do You Mean, 'It's the Relationship'? What's That Got to Do with Step-Parenting?" This article focuses on the difficulty in forming a good "WE" out of the natural "us" versus "them" tensions of the blended family. Practical ways of forming the "WE" are given that start with the marital relationship.

The third article, titled "Growing Up in a 'WE' Family" by Walter

[Haworth co-indexing entry note]: "Preface." Ludwig, David J. Co-published simultaneously in *Journal of Family Social Work* (The Haworth Press, Inc.) Vol. 4, No. 3, 2000, pp. xv-xvi; and: *Social Work and the Family Unit* (ed: David J. Ludwig) The Haworth Press, Inc., 2000, pp. xi-xii. Single or multiple copies of this article are available for a fee from The Haworth Document Delivery Service [1-800-342-9678, 9:00 a.m. - 5:00 p.m. (EST). E-mail address: getinfo@haworthpressinc.com].

Murphy, focuses on the benefit to children when the parents form a united front, developing a relationship that the children cannot manipulate.

The fourth article by William B. Knippa is titled "The Family Unit: PLACE, BASE or Both?" This article also focuses on the benefit to the children of a strong "WE" between the parents. Such a good, secure relationship that forms a united front allows children to have a healthy *place* to develop their personality, then a healthy *base* from which to launch their own lives.

The fifth article by Donald R. Bardill is titled "The Relational Systems Model: Reality and Self-Differentiation." This article focuses on the different relationships that form the realities of a person's life. This perceptive theoretical article shows how clients are empowered to live in the four realities as self-differented persons. The key to understanding human functioning comes from understanding the *relationships* that make up the person's life.

The final article by Charles J. Joanides, Harvey Joanning, and Patricia Keoughan is titled "Toward's an Understanding of Religious People's Perceptions and Lived Experiences of Religion and Spirituality: Implications for Marriage and Family Therapists." It focuses on the last of the four relationships delineated in the section of Bardill's article dealing with the spiritual reality. In their research, Joanides et al. find that religious people view their faith as interrelated and interconnected with the other realities of their experience.

The implication of all of these articles is that counselors see the relationships of the person's life, including the spiritual, as the key issues that can result in the most productive therapy work. The client normally does not see the relationship as the problem, since it is invisible. Focusing the client away from the other person and to the relationship as the problem can result in very productive therapy sessions.

David J. Ludwig, PhD, MDiv

It's the Relationship, Stupid!

David J. Ludwig, PhD, MDiv

SUMMARY. It is easy to blame the dysfunction of a family member on his or her behavioral patterns. I use the title, "It's the Relationship, Stupid!" not to talk down to family therapists, but to remind myself that the source of dysfunction is usually family relationships, especially the marriage relationship. This article gives several case studies for practical application of therapy techniques that focus on developing the "WE" of the family unit. One practical technique that I developed is a communication typology. The married couple (and family members) are divided into "Painters" and "Pointers." This typology explains much of the conflict and mis-communication that leads to the breakdown of the "WE." This article also presents dysfunction within the individual as a relationship problem and introduces the concept of the "spirit" of the individual as expressing the relationship the person has with self. *[Article copies available for a fee from The Haworth Document Delivery Service: 1-800-342-9678. E-mail address: <getinfo@haworthpress inc.com> Website: <http://www.haworthpressinc.com>]*

KEYWORDS. Family unit, family relationships, united front in parenting, "WE" language, communication typology, Painters and Pointers, conflict spiral, mood particles, forgiveness, prayer, blended family, single-parent family, internal conflict, double messages, inner spirit, overcontrol disorders, impulse-control disorders

---

David J. Ludwig is Chair, Department of Psychology and Sociology, Lenoir-Rhyne College, Hickory, NC. He is also a Licensed Psychologist and Assistant Pastor, Christ Lutheran Church, Hickory, NC.

[Haworth co-indexing entry note]: "It's the Relationship, Stupid!" Ludwig, David J. Co-published simultaneously in *Journal of Family Social Work* (The Haworth Press, Inc.) Vol. 4, No. 3, 2000, pp. 1-30; and: *Social Work and the Family Unit* (ed: David J. Ludwig) The Haworth Press, Inc., 2000, pp. 1-30. Single or multiple copies of this article are available for a fee from The Haworth Document Delivery Service [1-800-342-9678, 9:00 a.m. - 5:00 p.m. (EST). E-mail address: getinfo@haworthpressinc.com].

1

PART 1–FAMILY RELATIONSHIPS

I. The common mistake in working with families–not see the situation as a relationship problem

A. A Family unit is distressed

Alan's mother called, "I'm having problems getting my teenage son to obey. His behavior has been getting worse and worse. I think he needs help. Can you help him?"

I listened, then replied: "Sure, I think I can help."

"Good," mother quickly responded, "when can you see him?"

"Wait a minute," I replied, "will he tell me the truth?"

"Probably not," was the reply.

"Then you better come in, too," I advised . . . then added "Oh yes, bring your husband along so I can get the full picture."

I was waiting in my office. Alan sauntered in first, taking the choice seat and spreading his legs out to claim his territory. It was clear that he had quite an attitude and was used to controlling things. Then mother marched in, almost tripping over Alan's feet, selected a chair next to him and glared at Alan for not moving his feet. Alan put a little smirk on his face and looked away. Finally father came in, carefully walking past Alan's sprawled feet, choosing a chair that was furthest away . . . then he began staring at books in my office.

Mother looked at me, expecting me to begin. When I shrugged, she immediately took charge. Looking at Alan with obvious anger, she commanded, "Now you tell Dr. Ludwig what you did last night!" Alan gave his mother a look of disdain and with a defiant shrug, replied, "I don't have to do anything."

With that, mother quickly looked at father, angry that he was letting Alan get by with such disrespect. Father felt the look coming and let out a big sigh, turning his head away to look more closely at the book titles. Mother then looked at me, angry that I was not doing anything!

B. Each member of the family blames the other

Mother was convinced that the problem was father's lack of support. Father was convinced it was mother's harsh discipline. The son was convinced that he was being treated like a 9-year old. Each had private thoughts as to what would fix the problem, but all three were dead wrong.

C. The problem was the relationship between the parents!

Fifteen seconds had gone by. I knew exactly what the problem was. It was obvious that the relationship had broken down between mother and father. Alan was having a field day with the situation, knowing that he did not have to obey mom if dad did not support her! There was no united front . . . the WE had broken down (Ludwig, 1997; Quatman, 1997; Greene, 1984).

D. But the relationship is invisible, so this is not an apparent cause!

Realizing that the parents were blaming each other, I stepped in. I looked at Alan and asked, "You don't want to be here, do you?" "You got that right," Alan replied with all the swagger he could muster. "Good," I observed. "Get out . . . I don't need you."

With that Alan lost his powerful exterior and stammered, "But, but . . . " "I said that I do not need you," I repeated. "So get out." Alan turned into a little boy in front of my face. He stammered a few protests, but meekly got out of his seat and hesitantly walked out the door. He did not even slam the door when he left!

II. Reality is that the relationship(s) involved caused the distress

A. Each family member knows he/she did not want the distress to occur

I asked each of the parents if they liked the behavior of their son. The reaction was obvious. They agreed that the behavior was detrimental for the family and both suffered considerable internal distress when situations such as I had witnessed occurred. I then asked if either of them deliberately caused the situation to occur. "Why would I want to end up all torn up inside?" the father responded. It was obvious that neither wanted the distressed mood to occur.

B. Each person wants to change the behavior of another person with "If only he/she . . . "

"What would change things?" I asked.

The response came with no hesitation. "If only he would back me up," the mother began. "He always makes me do the dirty work. He refuses to discipline his son. His son has him wrapped around his little finger."

I asked the father if he agreed with that.

"Of course I don't," he burst out. "If only she would not react to every little thing he did. He does things just to get her upset. Boy, he really has her number!"

C. This is faulty thinking, for the source of distress (bad mood) is not the behavior of an individual

It was obvious to me that each was compensating for the actions of the other (Mash, 1984). She felt that he was letting their son get by with too much, so she had to be the one to hold the line. He felt that she was too harsh, so he had to be the one to give their son some freedom.

D. In reality, the mood grows out of the interaction process

I looked at the mother and said, "You are very angry right now. Most of your anger is at your husband's lack of support. You are trying very hard to control your son, but he does not support you!" Her eyes widened as she listened, then nodded in agreement as she glared at her husband with an "I told you so" look.

Then I addressed the father, "And you are very angry with your wife at this point. It's either her way or no way. She reacts, then expects you to back her up when you do not agree with her aggressive tactics." He looked at me with surprise, then shot a glance at his wife that meant, "You listen to him."

E. Since the "WE" controls the mood, getting the "WE" back between the two parents is the most powerful thing you can do in therapy

Then I softened and addressed both of them: "The problem that you are having is the breakdown of the united front. Your son is quite brilliant. He probably learned early in life how to split the two of you apart and now is able to do it at will. And it is getting dangerous, because he is stuck in the cracks and is way too immature for his age."

I then gave them "WE" homework (Ludwig, 1997). Addressing the mother, I instructed, "Don't you ever react to your son out of your own emotions. That is too dangerous. I saw the way he can make you angry. He knows you all too well. So when you notice something, *first* turn to your husband and ask to talk it through. Ally first, then correct your son as a WE!"

Addressing the father I instructed, "Don't you ever put your wife off with something like, 'What's the big deal?' or by turning away from her like I saw a few minutes ago. No, when she shares something she has noticed and is concerned about, treat her insight as a gift and immediately ally with her to form the WE. Add your own input, but make sure you are a united front when addressing Alan."

I practiced with them, role-playing their son, until I was confident they knew what they were to do. Then I sent them home, asking them to think WE and say WE anytime their son was involved.

They listened closely and were able to follow through because they did have a good relationship. They came back the next week and exclaimed that a miracle had happened. Much of the son's disrespect was gone and he even called the previous night to ask if he could stay out an extra 15 minutes since he was having trouble getting a ride home. Mother answered the phone and did it right. She said, "Just a minute, I will talk it over with your father and WE will get back to you."

I saw Alan for a few minutes that day also. He came in and tried to show his previous attitude when he complained, "Boy, you have ruined my life!" But the way he said it, it seemed more like he was thanking me, for now, instead of being over-focused on reacting to his parents, he could be a "kid" and grow up with the security that the WE gives. He was more interested in talking to me about his friends.

In fact, the way he described how he felt different made it sound as if a "switch" clicked on in his head when the "WE" between his parents came back into power. Alan just did not have the same desire to rebel (Ludwig, 1995).

III. Allowing the faulty perception that it is the other person's fault takes power away from family members

A. A sensitive issue comes up and the unity (WE) breaks down

Janet was very upset. "He pulled the same old trick last night," she began soon after they walked into my office. "We were not even finished with dinner when his mother walks in the door without knocking, as usual. The first think she did was to correct my daughter for eating with dirty hands. I pointed out that she had been playing outside in the red clay and that her hands had been washed, but all the red stain did not come off. Mother marched her to the bathroom anyway to wash her hands again. You can imagine how I felt with such disregard for what I said, so I said to my husband, 'Are you going to let her get by with that, Ben?' Instead of standing up for me, he just gave me that look and shook his head, telling me just to let it go." With this, she looked at her husband with a mixture of hurt and anger, but he only shook his head and looked away.

"How do you see the situation, Ben?" I asked. He responded, "If only she would not react to my mother like she does, things would be a lot more peaceful. Mother is just like that . . . she likes to take over. The best way to handle it is to ignore her. I don't see why Janet makes such a fuss over something as little as that." He said those last words with his teeth clenched slightly, covering some deep annoyance and anger.

B. As family members react with old (and usually predictable interaction), a negative spiral develops that pulls the mood down

It was obvious to me that this was not the first time that the subject of "mother" changed the mood between them. This was one of the sensitive issues that began soon after they met. He was still living with his mother when they met and there was an immediate clash over his attention, since mother had wrapped much of her life around her son. She lived alone for a few years after her divorce, but then persuaded her son to move in to "save some money." She seemed happy when he started dating, but soon was upset with the time he spent away from her.

After they married, Ben started sneaking around, visiting mother during work hours so that Janet would not know. Over their 10 years of marriage, clashes over his mother occurred almost every day, usually leaving both upset at each other. Picture each of these unresolved circumstances (Passions, 1975, p. 18) as contributing to the build-up of negative energy between Janet and Ben. Each time they walk away from each other, upset over his mother, more of this negative energy builds up. This energy can be pictured as collecting within the relationship as "mood particles" (Ludwig, 1989, p. 26).

The interaction in my office occurred after thousands of "mood particles" had built up in the area of "his mother." When these "mood particles" got activated, a predictable "conflict spiral" (Adler, 1996, p. 371) develops, resulting in a bad mood that can last for days.

C. Feelings are hurt and resentment builds as each family member feels both unjustly blamed and that his/her reality is not validated

After talking to Ben and Janet for a few minutes, it was obvious that they misunderstood each other in critical ways. The difference was that between "painter" and "pointer" (Ludwig, 1989, p. 43 and Ludwig, 1997, p. 22). These terms describe differences in communication style. Janet was a "painter" and Ben was a "pointer." Look at the following chart for a summary of the differences:

	PAINTER	**POINTER**
• **PERCEPTION**	Notices everything	Notices task at hand
• **CONSCIOUSNESS**	Keeps many things in mind	Focuses on one thing
• **DEFENSE OF SELF**	Vigilant so no surprises	Puts things in perspective
• **COMMUNICATION**	Paints a picture	Sticks to the point

[Note: There are many helpful typologies that describe differences in personality, such as the Myers-Briggs (Myers, 1962). The typology presented in this paper is designed to explain differences in communication style and give insight into the breakdown in communication between two people.]

How does a pointer misunderstand a painter? The pointer focuses on the first thing said and assumes that this is the point when it is only the first brush-stroke. Also the pointer is confused when the painter jumps around and the pointer thinks sequentially.

How does a painter misunderstand a pointer? The painter is looking for detail and misses the summarization that the pointer must start with. Also the painter is frustrated and starts digging for details by asking specific questions that forces the pointer to jump from file to file inside to give a summarizing answer.

How do you spot the cause of misunderstanding? Both must take a different look at reality!

1. Since the Pointer

    a. does not notice
    b. does not react emotionally
    c. wants to withdraw when there is tension
    d. shifts focus and gets involved in something else immediately
    e. rolls over and goes to sleep
    f. seldom brings things up.

THE PAINTER ASSUMES THAT THE POINTER
DOES NOT CARE!

THIS IS NOT REALITY!!!

The pointer cares just as much, but handles things differently!

2. Since the Painter

    a. Brings up things again and again
    b. Goes on and on about something
    c. Seems to overstate things for effect
    d. Will not let something go
    e. Gets emotionally upset over things
    f. Starts with an attack on the Pointer

THE POINTER ASSUMES THAT THE PAINTER IS TRYING
TO MAKE HIM/HER FEEL GUILTY!

THIS IS NOT REALITY!!!

The Painter is not blaming, but trying to connect!

D. There is TRUTH from different perspectives

PAINTER'S TRUTH

    1. The painter will react according to the feeling of the moment
    2. At any given time, there will be expression of that feeling
    3. That feeling cannot be put into perspective, or its expression will not be valid

POINTER'S TRUTH

    1. The pointer will react by summarizing feelings over time
    2. At any given time, the feeling will be put into perspective
    3. The pointer can be angry, but still validly say, "I love you"

PAINTER'S DISTRUST

1. The painter will pick up the non-verbal anger and know what the pointer is feeling
2. When the pointer gives the summary over time, it will not match with what the painter knows to be true
3. So the painter will say, "I don't trust what you say–you are not being honest"
4. But the pointer is being honest in the summary

POINTER'S DISTRUST

1. The painter will say "ever" and "never" to get the emotion out
2. The pointer will notice that the feelings change and the dramatic expression is no longer true
3. The pointer will say, I won't trust what you say next time ... you just make a big thing out of nothing, then forget it.
4. But the painter is being honest with what is going on at the moment!

E. Energy spent trying to change other family members is futile and builds resentment since other family members are doing the same!

1. Painters know that their mood will come back and they can feel close again if they can get the Pointer to understand what they are feeling
   a. So Painters use the strategy of presenting their reality in vivid color
   b. But the Pointer will only get more defensive and shut down
   c. So the Painter will paint the picture again and again with more emotional detail and emphasis, causing a spiral of defensiveness and withdrawal.

FASTEST WAY TO SHUT DOWN A POINTER:

- Interrupt the Pointer's logical flow
- Shift topic to related issue
- Keep digging for more information
- Try again and again to get your feelings across
- Ask, "WHY?" in an accusing tone of voice

---

2. Pointers know that their mood will come back and they can feel close again if they can set the record straight so that they are not blamed

    a. So Pointers use the strategy of correcting the Painter's reality

    b. But the Painter will only get more frustrated and upset

    c. So the Pointer withdraws to get things back into perspective

---

FASTEST WAY TO FRUSTRATE A PAINTER:

- Stop listening after the first sentence, assuming that was the point
- Get defensive and say, "That's not true"
- Correct the Painter's reality
- Suggest that the Painter is overreacting
- Shut down and withdraw

IV. Family members are empowered when they work on that which they can change!

A. Empowerment begins with the insight that the mood is controlled by the relationship

I use the "Painter/Pointer" distinction as a teaching device to show that the problem is not the other person, but misunderstanding in the relationship. I have found that about 85% of the couples I counsel can relate well to these categories. Also I found that about 75% of men are Pointers and about 75% of women are Painters, so there is a gender bias, but this is not a gender difference, since there are a significant number of male Painters and of female Pointers (Ludwig, 1989).

Once I taught Ben and Janet that they were misunderstanding each other as a Pointer and a Painter, I found them shifting the blame for the bad mood from the other person to the relational misunderstanding. Just that shift helped the mood between them considerably.

Each relationship has two halves that contribute to the interaction process–teaching family members how to work on their half of the relationship is empowering, for each family member has the power to stop the spiral (Ludwig, 1995).

I taught Ben how to work on his half of the relationship, rather than trying to change Janet. He began to realize that she could not ignore his mother like he could, since Painters notice everything and react emotionally to the situation. So he changed strategies. When Janet reacted, he asked her to tell him what she had observed, being careful to watch the whole picture being painted. He found that this would stop the downward spiral as Janet realized that she was being heard and could ally with him to do something about the situation.

I also taught Janet how to work on her half of the relationship, rather than trying to change Ben. She began to realize that Ben could not pick up and react to the things she noticed, since often he was focused on something else. When she noticed something, she was more willing to explain it to him, rather than be critical of his lack of reaction. She found this would stop his defensive reaction and alter the usual downward spiral. She also found that listening closely to his first words and asking for more detail gave him a chance to feel more a part of the process.

B. Practical ways to teach Painters and Pointers how to alter their strategies in the interaction process

How to help your pointer/painter spouse STAY CONNECTED!

A. For Pointers Only . . .

1. Do not focus on the first sentence, but sit back and watch a picture being painted, being fascinated with the colorful detail
2. Stop the impulse to set the record straight and do not solve anything
3. Allow expression of emotion . . . do not think the Painter is overreacting
4. Invite more expression . . . say, "Wow, tell me more about . . ."
5. Picture the Painter as juggling all those balls in consciousness and when you understand, you take one of those balls from the Painter

B. For Painters Only . . .

1. Listen closely to the first words spoken, for that will be the point
2. Use one of the Pointer's own words and ask for more information

3. Make it emotionally safe for the Pointer to share
4. Stop the impulse to bring up related subjects
5. Picture the Pointer's feelings as deeper in the file . . . if you want to get to emotional conversation, stay in the same file and make it safe!

C. For Both

1. Value staying connected more highly than

   a. setting the record straight (Pointer)
   b. getting your feelings across (Painter)

2. Send a signal of respect before saying anything

V. Goal is to get the "WE" back so that the mood will shift and things can then be talked through–the steps are

A. Do a reality check

We then talked over the situation of mother taking over and washing the daughter's hands. Both Ben and Janet agreed that at that moment they were upset at each other. Then I asked, "Did either of you want to feel the way you did?" The answer from both was a resounding, "NO!" "Well," I observed, "Then I guess it is clear that neither of you wanted the situation to occur."

But then I added that each had a different view of what would make it better. Janet was convinced that if Ben would stand up to his mother, things would get better. Ben was convinced that if Janet would not make a big deal out of it, things would be OK.

B. Be honest with the way you punish each other

I pointed out how the negative spiral developed. Janet was upset with mother's actions and sent a signal to Ben that she was annoyed with what had happened. Ben took her signal as a criticism of his lack of action and got defensive, shutting down and ignoring Janet. Janet, in turn, felt ignored and started to get more annoyed at Ben. The spiral had started. They needed to learn reconciliation and forgiveness (Hargrave and Sells, 1997 and Grizzle and Burton, 1992).

I gave them a series of steps that are part of this spiral:

A. When a Pointer feels unjustly criticized, a mood automatically sets in

   1. The perceived loss of respect leads to lowered sense of worth . . . the Pointer feels "put down"
   2. There is an immediate loss of energy . . . a "pout" sets in
   3. Non-verbal signals are given to diminish the importance of spouse
   4. These are units of ignoring (IGNORES) in 5-minute increments
   5. Six "IGNORES" = 30 minute pout
   6. These signals serve to balance the relationship, allowing the Pointer to gain respect back forcefully by "putting down" the spouse

B. When a Painter feels unjustly ignored, a mood automatically sets in

   1. The perceived loss of respect leads to lowered sense of worth . . . the Painter feels "put down"
   2. There is an immediate annoyance toward spouse's actions
   3. Verbal signals are given to diminish the importance of the spouse
   4. These are units of annoyance (ANNOYS) expressed in statements
   5. Six "ANNOYS" = six "IGNORES"
   6. These signals serve to balance the relationship, allowing the Painter to gain respect back forcefully by "putting down" the spouse

C. An unhealthy spiral develops, making the relationship turbulent and unsafe

   1. The "IGNORES" of the Pointer to gain back respect make the Painter feel unjustly ignored
   2. The "ANNOYS" of the Painter to gain back respect make the Pointer feel unjustly criticized
   3. The spiral can continue and build all evening

C. Stop blaming each other, but understand the spiral

After they understood this, I gave them the following homework to break this spiral. I knew that if each had the power to stop the spiral by a better understanding of the reality of the situation, the spiral would not end up in a bad mood for the better part of a week, like it had in the past.

Learning how to understand a painter's annoying comments

For Pointers Only:

1. Yes, the Painter is annoyed and is letting you know it
2. Yes, the Painter is doing it to put you down
3. But the Painter is really trying to feel close again!
4. These comments allow the Painter to get over the feeling of being unimportant to you
5. After a specific number of these comments, the his/her mood will come back and the Painter will be ready to reconnect!
6. If the Painter reconnects without doing this, there will be resentment for "giving in again"
7. So ultimately the Painter is trying to feel close again without building resentment . . . therefore:

    a. DO NOT take the annoying comments personally
    b. DO NOT spend your energy trying not to annoy by doing better next time
    c. DO NOT spend your energy trying to set the record straight
    d. RATHER, thank the Painter in your heart for trying so hard to feel close and connected to you again!!!!

Learning how to understand a pointer's ignoring behavior

For Painters Only:

1. Yes, the Pointer is hurt and is letting you know it
2. Yes, the Pointer is doing it to put you down by ignoring you
3. But the Pointer is really trying to feel close again!
4. This "pout" will allow the Pointer to get over the feeling of being unimportant to you.
5. After a specific amount of time, his/her mood will come back and the Pointer will be ready to reconnect!
6. If the Pointer reconnects without doing this, there will be resentment for "giving in again"
7. So ultimately the Pointer is trying to feel close again without building resentment . . . therefore:

    a. DO NOT take the "pouting" personally
    b. DO NOT spend your energy "walking on eggs" to keep the Pointer from shutting down

c. DO NOT spend your energy trying to get the Pointer to respond

d. RATHER, thank the Pointer in your heart for trying so hard to feel close and connected to you again!!!!

D. Put the "WE" above the "ME"

I taught Ben and Janet to work on a new "knee jerk" reaction when a situation with his mother developed. Since they were both blaming each other, I asked them to shift blame away from the other person and put it on the relationship (Ludwig, 1989). A word of prayer is of great benefit at this critical moment ((Butler, Gardner, and Bird, 1998). The cause of their hurt feelings would then not be the other person, but the breakdown of the WE of the relationship (Ludwig, 1997, p. 21). The following is a list I gave both of them:

THE MAGIC WORD, "WE"

1. Go back and talk over the last argument you had.
2. Go ahead and say what each of you is probably feeling. Say this phrase together, "It's your fault."
3. Now change your focus from the other person as the cause of the mood-shift to space between the two of you. Say these words together, "We have a problem."
4. Feel the difference in spirit or in the mood when blame is placed where it belongs–at the center of your relationship. Now you can unite against a common problem–the misunderstanding (and past mood particles) in this area of your relationship (Heaton and Pratt, 1990).
5. Now make this a knee-jerk reaction. Whenever you feel the mood shift and believe that it was the fault of your spouse, shift your perception from "you" to "we." So, put on your bathroom mirror, **NOT "YOU," BUT "WE."**

VI. To be able to put WE above ME, there must be a shift of consciousness from the usual cognitive/emotional reactions to the spiritual "heart"

When a person's feelings are hurt and their reality indicates clearly that things are not fair, the mood shifts and the process of getting even starts. Since the cognitive and emotional systems react to this perception of reality, a different (and more accurate) perception of reality must be constructed (Bardill, 1997).

To alter perceptions of reality, the person must go to a deeper level of consciousness represented by the spiritual "heart" (Ludwig, 1995, p. 66). As will be explained in more detail in the second section of this article, this deeper level of consciousness allows the person to "take the situation to heart."

In the client's experience, this involves a value judgment (Hargrave and Sells, 1997). So I asked both Ben and Janet to do a reality check the next time this spiral developed over some interaction with mother. "Which is more important," I asked them to ponder in their hearts, "your hurt feelings or the closeness you experience in your relationship?" When they are able to dig deep enough into their value system and realize that the marriage relationship is more important than the hurt feelings of the moment, a gradual, but real change in mood occurs as the concern for ME is replaced with concern for WE!

I gave the following check sheet to Ben and Janet to take home with them and follow when a bad mood spiral started developing–when Ben felt justified in "ignoring" Janet and she, in turn, felt justified in "annoying" Ben:

---

1. To be empowered, travel the 18 inches from the brain to the heart–or the 8 inches from the gut to the "heart" (Ludwig, 1995, p. 68).

2. Viewing the situation from the "heart" allows a different reality to emerge as concern for one's own situation ("ME") is changed to concern for the family unit ("WE").

3. Seeing things from the "heart" will allow the blame to be placed in the right place–the mood shifted because the "WE" broke down, so the relationship is at fault.

4. Such a real shift in perception enables you to react differently, thus altering the relationship's downward spiral (Adler, 1996, p. 371).

5. The end result can be talking things through and clearing the air, rather than the predictable bad mood and angry feelings toward each other.

I even told Ben and Janet that they would begin to appreciate the very thing about their spouse that has annoyed them the most. So I also sent home one more check sheet:

Appreciate the PAINTER FLASH

- Remember that the Painter keeps many things in consciousness at once

- When something is noticed, it gets registered along with all other similar things from the past
- Then, *flash* . . . the painter sees the whole situation clearly and reacts
- Not only that, but the painter can see into the future . . . what is small now will become big if nothing is done
- So the painter reacts as if the future is here!
- This is the painter's gift to the relationship . . . it can catch things before they become serious problems

Appreciate the POINTER FLASH

- Remember that the pointer can summarize many things into a single point
- When something happens, the pointer can look over the situation and pull things together
- Then, *flash* . . . the whole thing gets put into perspective
- Not only that, but the pointer can look at the bigger picture and see things for what they are
- So the pointer reacts as if this were the bigger picture
- This is the pointer's gift to the relationship . . . it can keep things from getting out of proportion

VII. Family problems are a result of the WE breaking down!

Take a look at the following family situations I worked with this past month. Ask yourself, "Where is the WE?" in each of the situations:

a. The family was in the den, each doing something different. Dad asked Billy (age 11) to get a tool for him. "Sure," came the eager reply and Billy jumped up to find what his father wanted. A few minutes later, mother asked Billy to help her with something. "Aw, mom," he replied, "why do I always have to do everything?" With that mother became more stern, "I said come here and help me." Billy sighed and looked at his father. Father rolled his eyes and Billy gives father that knowing look as he reluctantly gets up to help mother. *So, where's the WE? It is obvious from this exchange that father and son form a WE against mother! Not good for the family spirit!*

b. It was a blended family. Jim's 22-year old daughter was coming for the evening. When Sarah arrived, Jim jumped up to answer the door. He hugged Sarah and grabbed her hand, leading her to the couch. He listened intently as she gave him her more current problem. Candice, the step-mother, walked over to join the conversation, but Sarah deliberately turned her back to exclude her. When she sent a signal to her husband, he was annoyed and said that he was busy. Angry, Candice turned away, feeling left out. *So, where's the WE? It is obvious from this exchange that father and daughter form a WE against step-mother! Not good for the family spirit!* (Kelly, 1995).

c. Candice was only 4 years old, but it took hours to get her to go to sleep at night. Mother would put her down and warn her not to get back up. She would stay in bed for 5 minutes, then come out with some excuse. Mother would march her back to bed, only to have her return 5 minutes later with another excuse. After several more tries, mother would get angry and threaten Candice. Candice would then start crying and run to daddy. He would comfort her, giving mother an angry look for hurting his precious daughter. Mother would then get angry at father and demand that he put her to bed. Father would carry her to bed and stay in there for 1/2 hour as she had all sorts of things to ask him. After he came out of her room, she would be back in his lap in 5 minutes, wanting something else. After this happened several times, mother would finally intervene and spank Candice, putting her to bed and demanding that she never get out again! At this point, Candice would put up a good crying fit, leaving mother and father angry at each other. *So where is the WE? It is obvious that Candice is daddy's girl and has learned that she does not have to obey since daddy with take her side! The behavior problem is really caused by the breakdown of the WE.*

d. Melanie was 15 and was getting quite mouthy toward her father. They would usually get into an argument and he would send her to her room, sometimes without dinner. Mother would not interfere with the argument, but would wait until father was occupied with something else, then would slip into Melanie's room and comfort her, sometimes bringing her food. She would say that her father really did not mean what he said, but just had a hard day. *So where's the WE? It is obvious that mother and daughter form an underground WE against father's authority. In fact, much of father's anger is that he feels his authority undermined and much of mother's behavior is that she feels that it is either his way or no way.*

e. Belinda was a single parent, trying to deal with a 16 year old daughter. She was strict, fearful of Tammy's behavior. Tammy took off one day with her boyfriend and did not let her mother know where she was. Belinda was frantic and called her ex-husband. He responded that he did not blame her for leaving . . . for that was the reason he left her. She was too rigid and strict. Belinda then had the police out looking for her daughter and finally found her in another city. She went and got the daughter, but on the way home learned that her father knew all the time where she was. It was obvious that the father tacitly approved of the daughter's rebelliousness. *So where's the WE? The daughter was headed for serious trouble because the WE had disintegrated totally between her estranged parents* (Hanson, 1986).

VIII. A closer look at the Blended Family

Go back to the second example above–the blended family. Sarah had the power to defy her step-mother because the WE broke down (Kelly, 1995). I scripted a new way of handling the situation and role-played it with Jim and Candice. When Sarah came for her next visit, the first thing Jim was to do when the doorbell rang was to go over and hug Candice. Then the two of them were to go to the door together and greet Sarah with, "Hi, **WE** are glad you are here. Come on in." Then they were to sit down together, still holding hands, then look at each other and smile before addressing Sarah. During the conversation, they were to say "WE" often and look back at each other every 20 seconds.

When they returned the next visit, they said everything worked well for the first 27 minutes! They did exactly what I said and found a remarkable shift in Sarah's conversation. She admitted that she had messed up her life and needed to get on top of things. Her whine was gone and she was talking like an adult. But after 27 minutes, Jim forgot to look at Candice and got locked into Sarah's story of how hard her life was. Sarah caught the shift and reeled dad in! He started responding to her the old way and she started playing on his guilt like she had before. Candice felt the shift and tried to get Ben's attention, but he now started getting annoyed at her.

The WE broke down and the old mood was back. However, they now understood how important the WE was, so we practiced more to see if the WE could handle Sarah from now on. I even cautioned that Jim was not to talk to Candice alone for the next several months so that the WE would have a chance to grow stronger.

IX. A closer look at the Single Parent Family

Now go back to the last example above. Belinda was a single parent and Tammy had free reign of the situation because she formed the WE with her father. That gave her the power to defy her mother!

Belinda could not form the WE with her ex-husband (though that would be the best thing that could happen for the sake of the daughter). But she could work on her half of the relationship and not be as reactive to her daughter's defiance (Hanson, 1986). She still has a natural authority over her daughter, but Tammy knows all of her buttons. She can get her angry or make her feel guilty or anxious.

I taught Belinda how to change her half of the relationship with her daughter by utilizing the WE of the family unit. Whenever her daughter acted defiantly, instead of the usual anger and escalation, I taught her to pause and go to her "heart" and ponder what was best for the family. Then when she felt solid with her assessment, she was to look at her daughter with her "eyes connected to her heart" and say with depth and power, "It is not good for us that you talk to me that way. We will make a home here and I will do my best to take care of you. So you will not talk that way again."

I described to her that this was speaking from her heart with her love and concern for her daughter and for their family very much evident. I also showed her a video that modeled this situation (Ludwig, 1989, video 7c). She returned the next visit amazed at the change in her relationship with her daughter. "Still rocky, but I did not realize that my reaction was part of the problem. When I stopped being anxious and angry, Tammy also changed. I guess she realized that her defiance did not work anymore like it used to!"

PART II–THE RELATIONSHIP WITH SELF

I. The common mistake in working with individuals–not seeing internal distress as a relationship problem

A. Ben and Janet both felt personal distress

I worked with Ben and Janet separately for several sessions. Ben wanted to work on his anxiety over confrontation and Janet wanted to work on her feelings of powerlessness and depression.

B. Both felt that the problem was out of their control

Ben acknowledged that he "froze" when there was tension between Janet and his mother. "I just cannot do anything at the moment except withdraw," he concluded. Then he would rebel when Janet pointed out that he did not stand up to her, feeling that she was criticizing him and trying to control his behavior. So his only hope seemed to be to convince Janet to ignore mother so that there would be no tension.

Janet also felt helpless when the situation occurred. "I am powerless when it comes to getting his mother to stay out of our business," she concluded. His mother did not respect the boundaries she put up, so her only hope seemed to be to convince Ben to stand up for her.

C. Relationship with self is invisible, so blame other factors for bad moods

What Ben did not realize is that the rebelliousness he felt toward Janet's "control" was a result of internal dysfunction. Part of him never grew up, so the normal anger that would have given him the power to confront the situation turned into the desire to withdraw. There was something wrong with his relationship with self!

What Janet did not realize is that the powerlessness she felt was also a result of internal dysfunction. Part of her never grew up, so the normal power she should feel inside turned into anxiety and depression. There was something wrong with her relationship with herself.

II. In reality, there are three powerful forces within the individual

There are three powerful forces in the person's inner world. Freud (1949) used the terms "id," "ego," and "superego." Transactional Analysis (Goldhaber, 1976) uses the terms "parent," "adult," and "child."

Spirit-brain research indicates two somewhat separate consciousnesses inside, represented by the two hemispheres of the cortex of the brain. The two can communicate but seem to remain two separate ways of processing information.

If the person is right-handed, the left hemisphere probably contains the speech center and is called the dominant hemisphere. It processes information sequentially. In contrast, the right hemisphere is more spatially oriented and processes information more holistically.

A. Force #1–The "MIND"

The language ability of the left hemisphere allows the individual to think abstractly–to think about things in a detached fashion. This is what thinks back over what has happened and makes value judgments about the actions. This is the "force" inside that says, "Boy, that was really dumb." This is force #1. Let's call this force the verbal self or the "mind."

The "mind" is an essential force within one's consciousness. It is a good force that monitors direction for the person's life, evaluating right from wrong. It can detach from a situation and evaluate what is happening. It constantly monitors self.

The power of this "force" is the pervasive motivation to do the right thing. But this is also where the perfectionistic, "shoulds," and guilt feelings come from. The mind is powerful and relentless, constantly making the person aware of what should not have happened or of what should be done (Ludwig, 1995).

In Janet's case, her "mind" was over-developed, causing her to feel responsible for making sure things happened.

B. Force #2–The "BODY"

The right (or non-dominant) hemisphere does not detach, but stays more involved with the realities of the moment. This "force" is more expressive of one's impulses and feelings. When the individual has the distinct feeling, "I'm just not in the mood to clean things up," that is force #2 inside reacting. Let's call this force the non-verbal self or the "body."

The "body" is also an essential force within one's consciousness. It provides the impulse for action and gives emotional color to life. This passion–the zest for life and its fulfillment on moment-by-moment basis–is part of the energy of the body. This is where the impulse or the "want to" comes from (Ludwig, 1995).

In Ben's case, his "body" was over-developed, allowing him to walk away from responsibility and react in more rebellious ways to situations.

C. DOUBLE MESSAGES INDICATE INTERNAL CONFLICT

At any given time, both of these "forces" inside are active. In any conversation, the *mind* is dealing with what is being said and the *body is* dealing with the non-verbal aspects of the communication. If these two conflict, there is a double message. The person's *mind* may give a good, socially-acceptable response, "It's good to see you again," while at the same time the body might give a nonverbal negative message by adding a sarcastic tone. Thus, if there is not a good relationship with self, the person can't help but give out double messages and others will find it difficult to relate to that person.

When these two "forces" inside are in conflict, the energy is blocked and an internal "mood" develops. Much of the time is spent fighting self. Such internal struggles are common. The "mind" and the "body" have different ways of looking at things. The "mind" is aware of one's goals as it looks at the past and considers the future. The "body" is aware of one's needs at the moment. Often these two realities conflict with each other and need a third, mediating force to keep them working together in harmony.

D. THE "SPIRIT" IS THE "THIRD FORCE" THAT UNIFIES

Freud (1949, p. 14-16) used the term, "ego" to describe this force and Transactional Analysis (Goldhaber, 1976, p. 7) uses the word, "adult." I use the word, "spirit" as a description of the unifying force of the relationship, linking together separate forces into a living, creative unity. It is the organizing principle for relationships, forming basic attitudes, setting the atmosphere, and controlling communication. In Gestalt terminology, it is the "whole" that is "greater than the sum of its parts" (Sharf, 1996, p. 255). The oneness that couples experience that gives them greater energy for life is the two persons *plus* their relationship! Maslow (1954, p. 376) uses the word "synergy" to describe the energy of this force.

For both Ben and Janet, this internal, unifying force was not well-developed. Without this unifying force, they were trapped into reacting in their old, dysfunctional ways. It was accurate to describe their problems as coming from a damaged spirit.

The forces of the "mind" and the "body" are powerful and relentless and need to be controlled by a third force. The ***inner spirit*** is the unifying force of the soul that produces an organized consciousness. It is a deep and creative power, forming the organizing principle of the person's life–the person's basic identity and purpose. It is related to the person's faith (Vanden-Heuvel, 1986). It has the power to align the other two forces into a common direction, thus forming the basis of the "will" of the individual.

Since the inner spirit is not a static entity, but is involved in the process of relating, it cannot be directly measured. Yet its effects are quite evident in the mood and energy-level of the person. When the head and body work in harmony, there is a *good spirit* within (Sonnenberg and Ludwig, 1994). Genuine warmth and a caring attitude toward others mark the existence of a healthy inner spirit. This allows the person to "get into the spirit of" things, excited about different situations.

> *The person's spirit exists within the relationship he/she has with self–the cognitive and the emotional* plus *the relationship between these two forces within the person.*

Current cognitive and analytic therapy techniques focus on the inner life of the person and are of considerable help for the person's self-defeating thoughts and troubled emotional life. The missing ingredient in these therapies, however, is an understanding that consciousness is unified by an underlying spiritual force (Ludwig, 1995).

Without a healthy spiritual sub-structure to give direction and purpose, the personality loses its capacity for depth. The inner spirit, like a marriage relationship, can be weakened or damaged. Without a healthy mediating force, there is an inevitable power struggle inside with both sides trying to win and dominate the other. The lack of a strong organizing principle produces internal chaos and lack of self-control. Such inner battles are no fun!

In its battle for satisfaction, the body will settle for momentary pleasure–a pathetic substitute for the true fulfillment of its longing. In its battle for control, the mind will settle for following the letter of the law–also a pathetic substitute for the richness of life. Both of these give only surface satisfaction to the yearning of the soul, but miss the depth of life.

III. Empowerment of the individual begins with the insight that the mood is controlled by the internal relationship

1. Internal dysfunction is caused by a breakdown of the unifying force (spirit), leaving the other two powerful forces struggling for control of the personality.

2. The "cognitive" half is the "head" that fights for what the person "should" do (this can also be labeled the "verbal" side since this is the voice inside that the person hears).
3. The "emotional" half is the "body" that fights for what the person "wants to" do (this can also be labeled the "non-verbal" side since this is how the body reacts.
4. If the "head" wins, the person has an "**overcontrol**" disorder
5. If the "body" wins, the person has an "**impulse-control**" disorder.

A. Janet–Typical Overcontrol Disorder

Anxiety-based disorders occur when the person's "mind" (force #1) overcontrols the personality. This can only occur if the spirit (unifying force) is weakened or mis-formed so that it cannot take charge. Such problems often grow out of dysfunctional backgrounds where the child felt the need to please or to create a stable environment (such as in the case of alcoholic parents). This also occurs in guilt-inducing, highly critical, and perfectionistic background environments.

Such a person often is not aware of the impulse, disguising it or repressing it so as to keep in control of the situation. Guilt and anxiety are often the controlling factors. Guilt is usually anger turned inward and anxiety is the emotion detached from its source, diffused, and experienced as enhanced vigilance.

An overdeveloped "mind" produces heightened self-consciousness. The person is often afraid of making a mistake and thus can either become indecisive or will think back over a past situation again and again.

Janet grew up in a divorced situation with an alcoholic mother. At age 8, when the divorce occurred, she was already fixing her own meals and cleaning up the house. Since her mother would become verbally abusive when drunk, she developed the habit of scanning her mother's face to try to keep her from getting upset.

When she married, she quickly became the responsible person, aware of everything that needed to be done and worried much of the time. This prompted her to remind Ben constantly of things that needed to be taken care of. Of course, Ben interpreted this as a need to control him!

B. Ben–Typical Impulse-Control Disorder

Impulse-control disorders occur when the person's "body" takes control of the personality. This can only occur if the spirit (unifying force) is weakened or mis-formed so that it cannot take charge. Such a problem also grows out of dysfunctional backgrounds where there were poor boundaries. The child could then give in to the impulse, then get by with no consequences by being deceptive or emotionally volatile.

Such a person often is not aware of the consequences, feeling invulnerable as the acting out occurs. The person also feels justified in rebelling, since the other person is trying to "control" the situation.

Ben grew up with a father who had multiple affairs. When he was 11, his parents divorced after volatile arguments. His mother raised him, but was afraid he would turn out like his father, so she was constantly monitoring his actions. He developed a way of rebelling by being deceitful, just like his father, doing what he wanted, then hiding it from his mother. He would never confront his mother directly, but would just ignore what she had to say.

When he married, he quickly made Janet into his "mother" and started hiding things from her, feeling controlled by her personality. This set up an endless series of "mother/son" interactions that left Janet feeling frustrated and Ben feeling controlled.

C. Both felt powerless to change the pattern

In reality, the marriage produced an anxious 7-year old trying to control a rebellious 11-year old! The child usually gets "stuck" at the age-level the "WE" breaks down in their family of origin. Janet got stuck when her parents divorced at age 7 and Ben got stuck when his parents divorced at age 11. In fact, Janet appeared to be a precocious 7-year old, trying to get things to happen. Ben appeared to be stuck in pre-adolescence, rebelling at his mother's control.

Both blamed the other for the bad mood and felt powerless to change things. "If only Ben would grow up and take responsibility," was Janet's constant refrain. "If only Janet would 'chill' and not worry about everything," was Ben's constant thought.

Empowerment began for these two with the insight that they had gotten "stuck" as they were growing up. The powerful reaction each had to the other was their own internal dysfunction! This insight led to dramatic change in their interaction.

D. The Inner Spirit is the Creative Force as it takes Charge!

Both felt powerless to stop their usual feelings when the typical interactions occurred. With the insight, they had to learn how to change their internal reactions. To do this, they had to find that "place" inside that could take charge and stop the usual feelings from taking over. This "place" is the deepest area of consciousness where the personality is unified.

Do not assume that this "third force" within the person is a weak one and has to be handled with care. The unifying force is just as powerful as the others. Both Ben and Janet felt they were on the "outside," looking in when the bad moods struck. That's why they felt powerless to do anything different internally. They did not realize that there was a deep place within their consciousness that could take control!

To accomplish this, there must be a shift of consciousness from the usual cognitive/emotional reactions to the "heart." The "heart" is not a physical location, but represents this deeper center of consciousness that most people experience in the heart area (Ludwig, 1995).

1. To be empowered, the individual must travel the 18 inches from the brain to the "heart"–or the 8 inches from the gut to the "heart."
2. Viewing the situation from the "heart" allows a different reality to emerge as concern for the "should" or "want to" exclusively is changed to concern for the good of the whole individual.
3. Seeing things from the "heart" changes control of the personality from the individualized forces of the "head" or the "body" to the unifying force of the spirit.
4. Such a real shift in perception enables the person to react differently, thus altering the internal relationship's downward spiral.
5. The end result can be a deeper understanding of self and an empowering, rather than the predictable bad mood and inner distress.

IV. Working on one's internal dysfunction makes the person's half of the relationship more functional!

A. "Growing up" requires a change of strategy

Both Ben and Janet were still using childhood strategies in dealing with the situation with his mother. Ben allowed his "body" to take over and rebel by ignoring her. Janet allowed her "head" to take over and try to change Ben's behavior. It was easy for me to picture the anxious "7-year old" trying to make her "11-year old" brother obey her. That seemed to be the picture of the marriage relationship!

I worked with Ben's withdrawal behavior. He actually was very angry with his mother for her interference, but used his anger in an inappropriate way by rebelling behind her back. I had noticed that Ben would not look at Janet when she was upset at him. I was convinced that Ben would "grow up" the moment he could look directly at his mother and set boundaries with her. So I practiced with his relationship with Janet. I asked Janet to role-play being upset with him. I stopped and asked what he felt.

He first shrugged his shoulders and said, "Not much," but I saw the tension around his lips. I made him aware of this tension and ask him to exaggerate the tension (Passions, 1975, p. 65) and amplify the feeling, looking directly at Janet. There came a brief explosion of anger that sounded more like a temper-tantrum. Ben immediately withdrew. I now asked him to bring that anger to his heart. I had taught him already how to "move" the feelings in his "gut" the 8 inches to his "heart." I asked him to look at Janet again and tell her his anger. This time his voice was strong and mature as he said, "Janet, you do not have to talk down to me. But I want to know more about your frustration. Tell me what you are feeling." This took Janet by surprise! She talked about her feelings of powerlessness and for the first time, she felt heard!

Then it was Janet's turn. I knew she hid her feelings behind her analysis of the situation, so I asked her to stop and travel the 18 inches from her head to her heart. "Don't try to fix the situation," I ask her, "But now tell me what you need."

Immediately Janet's face softened as she felt safe to be vulnerable. She looked at Ben with a softness I had not seen before and asked him to help her with the situation with his mother. I saw compassion in Ben's face that I also had not seen before as he began to understand her feelings of powerlessness. This conversation was so different from the usual pattern when the subject of "his mother" came up that I called this a true "heart-to-heart" talk.

B. Getting both halves of the relationship functional helps the "WE" of the marriage

I gave them specific instruction on how to handle the way mother-in-law crossed the boundaries of their family. I told them to ask Ben's mother in a kind way to sit down and have a discussion. Both were to make sure that they stayed in their "heart" during the conversation.

Then Ben and Janet were to look at each other and smile (see Ludwig, 1989, video 7a). This controls the mood and keeps the WE strong. Then they were to look back at his mother and Ben was to say, "Mother, **we** need to talk about what happened yesterday." Then they look back at each other and smile. Janet picks up the same thought and also uses "we," "Yes, we have been talking about the way you washed our daughter's hands after we explained that they were clean." Then they look back at each other and smile. "We would appreciate it if you would respect what we say in regard to our daughter" Ben was to say, then look back at Janet again and smile. "Do you have any questions with what we ask you to do?" Janet was to conclude.

Ben was very anxious about doing this, not wanting to offend mother, but he saw the wisdom and agreed to do it. He had new confidence from what he had just felt when he stayed in his "heart" with Janet (Call and Heaton, 1997). We role-played a few times, then they went home to sit mother down. Ben called that night, quite relieved and happy. "What did mother say?" I asked. He replied, "Actually very little . . . she just said, 'OK,' and went onto something else. But I can see she knows her boundaries a lot better!'"

REFERENCES

Adler, R. and Towne, N. (1996). *Looking out, looking in*. New York: Holt, Rinehart and Winston.

Bardill, R. (1997). *The relational system model for family therapy: Living in the four realities*. Binghamton, NY: The Haworth Press, Inc.

Butler, M., Gardner, B., and Bird, M. (1998). Not just time-out: Change dynamics of prayer for religious couples in conflict situations. *Family Process*. 37, 451-457.

Call, V. and Heaton, T. (1997). Religious Influence on Marital Stability. *Journal for the Scientific Study of Religion*, 36, 382-392.

Freud, S. (1949). *An Outline of Psychoanalysis*. NY: Norton and Company.

Goldhaber, G. (1976). *Transactional Analysis*. Allyn and Bacon.

Greene, R. and Kolevzon, M. (1984). Characteristics of healthy families. *Elementary School Guidance and Counseling*, 19, 9-18.

Grizzle, A. and Burton, L., (Ed), (1992). *Religion and the family: When God helps*. New York: The Haworth Press, Inc.

Hanson, S. (1986). Healthy single parent families. *Family Relations: Journal of Applied Family and Child Studies*, 35, 125-132.

Hargrave, T. and Sells, J. (1997). The development of a forgiveness scale. *Journal of Marital and Family Therapy*, 23, 41-63.

Heaton, T. and Pratt, E. (1990). The effects of religious homogamy on marital satisfaction and stability. *Journal of Family Issues*, 11, 191-207.

Kelly, P. (1995). *Developing healthy stepfamilies: Twenty families tell their stories.* New York: The Haworth Press, Inc.

Ludwig, D. (1997). *The power of WE* (video). St. Louis: Concordia Publishing House.

Ludwig, D. (1989). *Renewing the family spirit* (book and video). St. Louis: Concordia Publishing House.

Ludwig, D. (1995). In *The missing ingredient: The spiritual dimension of counseling.* St. Louis: Lutheran Family Association and Concordia Publishing House (also published by Open Book in Adelaide, Australia, 1999).

Mash. E. (1984). Families with problem children. *New Directions in Child Development*, 24, 65-84.

Maslow, A. (1954). *Motivation and Personality.* NY: Harper and Brothers.

Myers, I. B. (1962). *Manual for the Myers-Briggs Type Indicator.* Palo Alto, CA: Consulting Psychologists Press.

Passons, W. (1975). *Gestalt approaches in counseling.* NY: Holt, Rinehart and Winston.

Quatman, T. (1997). High functioning families: Developing a prototype. *Family Therapy*, 24, 143-165.

Sharf, R. (1996). *Theories of psychotherapy and counseling.* NY: Brooks/Cole.

Sonnenberg, R. and Ludwig, D. (1994). *Living with Purpose* (video). St. Louis: Concordia Publishing House.

Vanden-Heuvel, A. (1986). Faith development and family interaction. *Dissertation Abstracts International*, 46, 4003.

What Do You Mean,
"It's the Relationship"?
What's That Got to Do with Step-Parenting?

Alex Opper, MSW, LCSW

SUMMARY. In blended families, the two parents have a unique challenge to develop a united front ("WE") in the face of "us" and "them" thinking. Without such a united front, the children will naturally manipulate the situation and further divide the blended family. The key to successful step-parenting is the development of a solid "WE" between two parents so that the whole family works together as a unit. Practical suggestions are given for development of this united front so that step-parenting can become a positive experience. *[Article copies available for a fee from The Haworth Document Delivery Service: 1-800-342-9678. E-mail address: <getinfo@haworthpressinc.com> Website: <http://www.haworthpress inc.com]>*

KEYWORDS. Step-parenting, healthy stepfamilies, "WE" of the blended family, "WE" boundaries, forgiveness

Step-parenting usually conjures up a negative image. Society promotes this image in folklore, the press, TV and the movies. This is especially significant in light of the fact that there are more children being raised in stepfamilies than any other form of family constellation. With this expectation of negativity where does one look to gain a sense of trust, hope and control when working with blended families?

Alex Opper is affiliated with the Counseling Services of Catawba County, Hickory, NC.

[Haworth co-indexing entry note]: "What Do You Mean, 'It's the Relationship'? What's That Got to Do with Step-Parenting?" Opper, Alex. Co-published simultaneously in *Journal of Family Social Work* (The Haworth Press, Inc.) Vol. 4, No. 3, 2000, pp. 31-35; and: *Social Work and the Family Unit* (ed: David J. Ludwig) The Haworth Press, Inc., 2000, pp. 31-35. Single or multiple copies of this article are available for a fee from The Haworth Document Delivery Service [1-800-342-9678, 9:00 a.m. - 5:00 p.m. (EST). E-mail address: getinfo@haworthpressinc.com].

Kelly (1995) gives that sense of hope with his book, *Developing Healthy Stepfamilies.* In this book, he gives examples of twenty stepfamilies that were able to form a good blended family unit.

A contemporary example can also be seen in Mark McGuire. He is well-known for his towering home runs as he plays baseball for the St. Louis Cardinals. His son is being raised by his former wife and her husband. However, he actively supports his former wife's new family, freeing the child to be loved openly by all parents in his life. By his attitude, Mr. McGuire has empowered this step-parenting relationship so that his son can be reared in a healthful environment.

My father's experience as a child was much different. He was neglected and verbally abused by his stepmother. When I learned of this, I was confused, since I was raised to love and respect "grandma." Most of my confusion and resistance continued until I became a stepson. After my mother's death, my father married "Mom Carol." I was in my forties.

Mom Carol and Dad were married nearly ten years and she modeled a wonderful step-parent. The core of this was their relationship. In the book *Beyond the Best Interest of the Child* (Goldstein et al., 1979), the major insight is that children are loyal as they bond to their parents:

> Unlike adults, who are generally capable of maintaining positive emotional ties with a number of different individuals, unrelated or even hostile to each other, children lacked the capacity to do so. They will freely love more than one adult only if the individuals in question feel positively to one another. Failing this, children become prey to severe and crippled relationships in love and confidence. (Ch. 2, p. 12)

For the past six years, I have been a stepfather myself. For those six years, my wife and I have parented four children, three of mine biologically and one hers biologically. I expected our blended family to be easy because I loved both my wife and stepdaughter and they loved me. But it was not easy. I went from the "sugar-coated" image of my dad's early experience to confusion.

I wanted it to work so badly. But the forces we faced were far beyond what I expected. The loyalty to your own child (children) is so powerful, that when things deteriorate, its "us" against "them." We were in considerable difficulty when we finally discovered that the new "WE" that my wife and I formed had to be stronger and more important than the natural "us" and "them" forces that constantly battle.

What this means is that anyone considering forming a blended family must be aware of the importance of the new "WE" that is formed. The new marriage relationship must be strong enough to blend both previous families together! Otherwise the "us" and "them" forces will tear the new family apart!

For example, I was reared in a patriarchal family. My wife was reared in a matriarchal family. Alcoholism was a large factor in both of our families. I was married for nearly eighteen years the first time. She had been married for ten. Both of us attempted to validate ourselves in the first marriage through our caretaker roles.

Ten years ago we met and six years ago we married, bringing up our children ages 13, 15, 16 and 17 together. During the four-year courtship we focused heavily on all those things we were doing correctly as single parents. We got married, sold our houses, built a new one, sent the eldest daughter off to college, graduated two more from high school and sent them to college, got the youngest through high school and into the Marines.

Indeed, we are proud of this, yet during this time the relationship was neglected. We reverted back to our roles as caretakers of our respective children but not of ourselves. We attempted to validate ourselves through our children. We worked very hard to make sure our children had what we did not and to make matters worse, we attempted to compensate for the absent parent. Resentment grew and flourished.

As you work with those considering a second marriage and combining two families or as you work in a therapeutic relationship with a blended family, there is one key concept that must be explored, digested and allowed to evolve. *The "WE" of the new family unit must be more important than all other concerns.*

Give the following list to your counselees. Use it as a way of emphasizing the importance of the "WE."

1. Use the word, "WE," in all discipline situations.
2. When you are together, look at each other and smile, then look back at the child and say, "We have decided that . . ."
3. When you are alone with the child (or children), say, "I will check with ___ and WE will get back to you." Or if you know what the decision is, say, "We agree that you should . . . "
4. To build the WE, recognize the different gifts each of you bring to the relationship. See your differences as gifts, not as differences that undermine what you are trying to do!

5. Work together and value each other's input as you establish rules and boundaries (Fine et al., 1998). Then make sure you enforce them together!

6. Value time together as a couple. Feed the marriage relationship. Energize the relationship to empower it through the hard times. Go out on dates. Get the kids out of the house. Do not wait until the kids are grown up to take a break and enjoy being with each other.

7. Do not be critical of the absent parent (McIvor, 1998). The children will take this as an opportunity to form an "us" against "them" situation that will be deadly for the WE of the blended family.

8. Do not be critical of a former spouse. Stepchildren are not rubber bands to be pulled and stretched, and expected to give and take when it comes to their absent, biological parent. Your children are fifty percent you and fifty percent of the non-custodial parent. If you rear that child in an environment where they feel that fifty percent of themselves is of no good value, what does that do to their self-esteem?

9. Another crucial issue is forgiveness. Have you forgiven yourself for the mistakes you have made? Have you asked for and received forgiveness from your partner? In any relationship, there are mistakes and if the relationship is to survive, it is so much more difficult when old issues surface and are never put to rest through forgiveness. Your faith can be an asset. God can help you forgive.

10. Look at your individual expectations of the blended marriage and come up with a mutual picture of your marriage. If you were reared by parents who had a good marriage, your expectations will be for a good marriage. You will have some direction as to what made their marriage a good one. However, what if your parents were alcoholics or workaholics? What if your parents hid behind you in your life, rearing you in an environment of simmering resentment, hostility, or marital apathy? In that case, you may have to an inherent view that marriage really isn't all that great; you may not expect a good one for yourself.

As a therapist, I work with many couples who have been in a variety of marriages, who would rather stop working on the marriage at the point where the relationship reaches to the level of their expectations. They begin divorce again, go through the whole process and divorce again, with no understanding that they can evolve in the relationship, re-write their "directions" and grow in their marital expectations (Keshet, 1990).

Often, when a couple is at the point where they feel that they can no longer evolve, children in the stepfamilies become scapegoats. This is to absorb the tension away from the parents in order to avoid more family breakup though it may be to "protect their parent from the spouse, whether perceived or actual abuse." Nathan W. Ackerman, in his book, *Treating the Troubled Family* (1993), states that "it is amazing how often in the course of family therapy the children respond with a striking improvement in their adaptation as the burden of displayed conflict is transposed to its prime source, conflict in the parental and marital pair."

This prime source to feed the blended family is indeed the marital relationship. This forms the basis of the "WE" that brings the disparate parts of the blended family together into a new unity. Address the issues of the children being in a step-parent relationship, teach forgiveness, to move onward.

The "WE" grows out of the relationship established by the new couple, with all or its emotional wounds and baggage. It can be formed to become the basis of a healthy blended family in which all family members feel safe and secure. Empower your clients to be a couple first, and then to parent their children as a team.

REFERENCES

Ackerman, N. (1993). *Treating the troubled family.* Northvale: Jason Aronson Publishers.
Fine, M., Coleman, M., and Ganong, L. (1998). Consistency in perceptions of the step-parent role among step-parents, parents, and stepchildren. *Journal of Social and Personal Relationships, 15*, 810-828.
Goldstein, J., Freud, A., and Solnit, A. (1979). *Beyond the best interest of the child.* New York: The Free Press.
Kelly, P. (1995). *Developing healthy stepfamilies: Twenty families tell their stories.* New York: The Haworth Press, Inc.
Keshet, J. (1990). Cognitive remodeling of the family: How remarried people view stepfamilies. *American Journal of Orthopsychiatry, 60*, 196-203.
McIvor, R. (1998). Working with step-parents. *Journal of Family Studies, 4*, 107-108.

Growing Up in a "WE" Family

Walter Murphy, PhD

SUMMARY. When couples choose to parent as a unit (the couple as WE) rather than as autonomous individuals, they and their children both benefit. The current article details some ways that parents can further expand their "couple as WE" into a "family as WE" with active parents and socially perceptive children. The article also discusses ways that family members can start and maintain a family dialogue. *[Article copies available for a fee from The Haworth Document Delivery Service: 1-800-342-9678. E-mail address: <getinfo@haworthpressinc.com> Website: <http://www.haworthpressinc.com>]*

KEYWORDS. Family as a "WE," active parenting, discipline styles, "WE" language, united front of parents, moral code, authoritative parenting style, family togetherness, family ties

The lead article in this book deals with the effects on the family of the parental couple as "WE." Ludwig emphasizes that a family is a set of inter-relationships, and that the relationship between the parents sets the tone for the relationships between the parents and the children (Ludwig, 2000). The couple as WE are more cohesive and share responsibilities. As WE, the couple are also more effective as parents, since they work together to develop rules for the family and reinforce each other's parenting decisions. Change is possible mainly when the parents function as WE in their hearts *as well as* in their heads. This suggests that WE may also go beyond the parental couple itself–that WE can include the entire family.

Many newspaper and popular magazine articles have lamented the demise of the nuclear family, blaming the decline on societal changes, problems in the government, a lack of church leadership, and a continu-

Walter Murphy is Assistant Professor in Psychology, Lenoir-Rhyne College, Hickory, NC.

[Haworth co-indexing entry note]: "Growing Up in a 'WE' Family." Murphy, Walter. Co-published simultaneously in *Journal of Family Social Work* (The Haworth Press, Inc.) Vol. 4, No. 3, 2000, pp. 37-50; and: *Social Work and the Family Unit* (ed: David J. Ludwig) The Haworth Press, Inc., 2000, pp. 37-50. Single or multiple copies of this article are available for a fee from The Haworth Document Delivery Service [1-800-342-9678, 9:00 a.m. - 5:00 p.m. (EST). E-mail address: getinfo@haworthpressinc.com].

al focus on negative events by the media. While these all contribute to the changes in family life seen in the late twentieth century, one source of the problem that has not been discussed as much is the lack of preparation of couples to begin their parental obligations. It is interesting that, prior to marriage, couples may be mandated by their faith community to undergo premarital counseling, which has been shown to reduce the rate of marital problems and divorce (Stanley, Markman, St. Peters, & Leber, 1995). Few couples, however, seek any counseling or help before having children unless infertility or family medical history are issues. Furthermore, with the increase in blended families (when divorced parents marry and bring together children from different marriages), the problems involved in raising children are expanding.

There is a strange contradiction in the way that society and modern parents interact. Many people believe that raising children is simple and requires little knowledge–anyone can raise a child; no training or experience is necessary. (Some others disagree, suggesting that whole communities be involved in the childrearing.) However, the American infatuation with authorities and specialists suggests that when starting something new, it is critical to seek outside help, especially from those with expertise or at least an advanced education in the field. New parents themselves are unsure how well they can cope, so they look for authorities, often in popular books or television shows. There are many books on raising "healthy" children, and, interestingly, quite a few of the authors of these books disagree on fundamental issues such as discipline or the effects of divorce on children. A few of the authors also do research, but the majority base their suggestions on their professional experiences, which vary. The current article examines only the research that studies parent-related issues, not that on child-related issues.

A definition of *the family as WE* might explain the phrase in this way: the family as WE consists of three elements: (1) active parents with (2) perceptive children, engaged in (3) appropriate dialogue with each other. Each of these elements is described below.

WHAT IS ACTIVE PARENTING?

Being Aware of Issues the Child Is Facing and Anticipating Problems the Child May Encounter

Children need active parenting rather than reactive parenting. It is much better for parents to anticipate possible problems and to work to prevent them rather than to deal with them as they arise. No matter how smart the child is or how carefully the parents structure the environment when they are with their children, there is a great deal of time that children spend unsupervised by parents. How comfortable are most parents that their child knows what to do in dangerous situations such as crimes attempted against them, peer pressure to engage in risky behaviors, or natural disasters? The parents want their children to be prepared to deal with problematic situations as they have been trained, just as they might teach them about safety in the event of a home fire. Talking and modeling behavior are critical–children will learn to do what parents DO, not what they SAY, so parents must follow their own rules. It may be worthwhile to look to authorities for basic knowledge, but the application of that knowledge to the family is the parents' responsibility.

Parents need to be aware of a child's abilities at various ages and not set their expectations of the child at too low or too high a level. The individual ability of each child is special, and siblings' personalities vary from each other or from what the parents would like; parents' valuing all their children's distinctive characters shows their children that they are loved and fosters more optimal development of children's abilities.

Recognizing and Accepting Their Individual Differences

Parents also tend to believe that, if they are doing well raising one child, they can use the same strategies on another child and those will work–frequently they are disappointed. Children should be treated in the manner most appropriate to their own actions. Individual differences between children may mean that different parenting skills are needed for each child, even when that leads to problems. For example, the oldest child might not want to stay out too late, so parents do not need enforce a curfew. When the next oldest stays out much later, parents are forced to set a curfew. This not only frustrates the parent who has to rethink parenting strategies, but also may bring on an argument with the younger child about why the older child had no curfew. Explaining logically to the younger child why different techniques are used for different children may help nurture a satisfying sense of uniqueness in that child. Acceptance of individuality becomes most critical when children are adolescents, as they are seeking to separate from the family and to find a distinctive identity. Parent-child conflicts heighten during early adolescence, which is perhaps the reason that families are referred more often for family therapy during this time of a child's life (Young, 1991). The parent-child conflict serves a useful role by allowing adolescents the opportunity to define their own beliefs.

Adjusting Discipline and Reasoning Styles as the Child Ages

As a child develops, strategies that once worked well may become less effective. Adolescents reason like adults, so it is necessary to explain rules to them. They also can use the information given to them to help form their own responses to situations. However, reasoning is not a useful tool with fairly young children and may even backfire as a behavior modification technique. A three-year-old has too little experience of the world to understand why she should eat her peas "because a homeless child wishes he had peas to eat." She may even volunteer to bring her peas to the homeless child. If parents wish to give an explanation, a better one may be that peas help her grow up healthy. The egocentric toddler deals better with self-related explanations than abstract, other-related ones. Research on parenting styles suggests that an authoritative parenting style (one in which rules are enforced but with age-appropriate explanations by warm parents) is most effective in developing self-competent children (Baumrind, 1980). However, at some ages combinations of authoritative parenting and other styles may be more effective. Authoritarian parenting (rules are enforced without much explanation) may sometimes work better with very young children, who may not understand the explanations, or permissive parenting (less rigorous rule enforcement) may better suit adolescents, who need opportunities to self-regulate.

Getting Involved with Children's Activities (Television Watching, Sports, Clubs, Computer Use)

In general, perhaps as a result of increased work responsibilities, parents are spending less time with their children than they were previously (Piotrkowski & Hughes, 1993). It seems likely that parents are not watching television with their children. Many households now have multiple television sets, so parents and children watch television separately. This means that parents are not there to interpret or at least monitor their children's television programs. New television sets may contain the v-chip, but that would not be necessary if parents were present to oversee what their children watch. Parents should watch their children's programs at least periodically. That would allow them to comment on the programming and help the child internalize the parents' moral code regarding the programming.

Unfortunately, depictions of parents on television, especially on situation comedies which are considered *family programming* frequently show neurotic or ineffectual people whose children are more wise and organized than they are. Also women and ethnic minorities are often depicted in stereotypical ways. If parents and children watch television together, parents could mitigate the negative stereotypes shown. In addition, parents should get involved in sports, social, and church activities with their children. Parents themselves benefit from this type of involvement. Research by Coltrane (1990) reports that parents who are involved in their children's lives on a frequent basis feel that they themselves become more empathetic, more tolerant, more self-confident, and more responsible.

Developing into a Couple as WE

Although people often list marriage as the major step in early adult development, adjusting to parenting may be more difficult. Research suggests that the level of a couple's satisfaction in their marriage begins to decline after children are born and does not begin increasing again until children leave the home (Anderson, Russell, & Schumm, 1983). While the decline itself may be small, the stress is probably caused by having another person to pay attention to besides the marriage partner. Keeping the relationship between the partners as strong as possible (maintaining the WE) will help provide social support for their parenting efforts and will provide them with someone to turn to as an outlet for struggles in parenting. Parents will need to adjust their own relationship as their children age.

One simple strategy for parents is always to act as a team. Husband and wife become partners in childrearing. Parents should start using the word *WE* as they make the transition to parenting and keep using WE in their parental roles. Some examples might include: *We are expecting a child in June. I can't make that decision now. When your mother she gets home from work, we will discuss it. We appreciate your concern, Mom, but please understand that Tom and I must discipline our children as we see fit.* This prevents children from undermining the authority of one parent with that of another. In some amicable divorces or for single parents who have moved back in with their parents, keeping some sort of WE can provide necessary social support. The former spouse (Arditti, 1992) or a grandparent (Beck & Beck, 1989) can serve as the partner in the WE. When an issue or problem arises with a child, allying with the partner should be the first step in resolution. Then the partners can consider the child's welfare together and work out a solution. The solution should be presented as a joint effort of the partners, for example, *We've discussed it and decided that you cannot go to your friend's post-prom party. Your mother and I both feel that, although you're old enough to attend a prom and we're thrilled you are going, you are too young to cope with some of the activities that may arise at that type of unsupervised party.* Using a logical explanation and keeping a united front will reduce the likelihood that a child will continue to object to the parents' decision. Parents are usually the best judges of what difficulties their child is prepared to deal with.

Relying Primarily on the WE for Help Rather Than on an Authority

Many parents today tend to want to put too much responsibility for childrearing into the hands of others, especially authorities. Instead of parents advising their children on appropriate sexuality, children learn at school in health classes. Instead of parents educating children about the hazards of drug abuse, programs like D.A.R.E. are used. Research on social learning reports that children are most likely to follow the example of people who are nurturant toward them (Bandura, 1989), and few teachers or community officials are as nurturant as a child's own parents. There are a number of other problems involved in relying on authorities for information on how to raise children, including the loss of parental authority, inappropriate generalization of research, and the possibility that children, especially adolescents, may see the parents as inadequate.

Some parents have argued for laws such as those requiring v-chips for new televisions, built-in restrictions for computer access on the Internet, and parental consent for teenagers to obtain abortion. While lawmakers are accommodating them, those same lawmakers resist similar types of regulations on businesses. The argument against regulating businesses has been that regulation by laws takes away independence and self-reliance from the business owners. The same argument could be applied to regulations regarding parenting, however. Why should parenting decisions be legislated?

A second problem with reliance on authorities is that the research reported in their books are often generalities, not appropriate for specific individuals. It is common for research in the social sciences to be done at group level. The inappropriate generalization of such research to individuals can be detrimental, but that fact is rarely emphasized in popular books. For example, Gray's work on differences in style between males and females (for example, Gray, 1992) uses results of group studies, and many people do not fit that set of molds. Also psychology research that has been popularized lately tends to advocate biological origins of problems rather than societal ones, and people tend to think of biological personality problems as unalterable.

A final problem with parents relying on authorities rather than each other is that it suggests that parents themselves are not knowledgeable, which may decrease their children's reliance on the parents' rules and beliefs. Parents need to allow themselves to make decisions based on their best judgment, even when their decisions go against popular ideas of what is correct. Although this belief is not widespread, at least one prominent child-care authority (Spock & Rothenberg, 1992) suggested this in his popular childrearing books. In fact, parents' maintaining consistent ideology in the face of social change or disfavor strengthens the sense of the family as a cohesive group with shared goals (an ideal for the family as WE). This creates a high degree of intimacy within the family (Maccoby, 1980).

In the past, the authority relied on often was the extended family, as is still often the case in many parts of the world. In the late twentieth century, our American society has gotten very mobile, which means more employment and learning opportunities, but fewer adults living near their parents and siblings than previously. While some people choose to diverge from the childrearing practices they were raised with, the extended family is often an ideal source of authority. This is true partly because the parents' own lives are evidence that the strategies used by previous generations were successful and partly because the extended family usually supports the parents' beliefs, since they share them. Some segments of American society (such as minority groups) rely on extended family members, who can especially help reduce the strain on young or single parents (Harrison, Wilson, Pine,

Can, & Buriel, 1994). The extended family can be a source of help even across the miles, due to advances in communication technology.

HOW CAN PARENTS HELP THEIR CHILDREN TO BECOME MORE PERCEPTIVE?

Talking with Them and Listening to What They Have to Say; Especially Talking Often with Them About What Is Right and What Is Wrong

Parents need to talk more with their children–even adolescents desire warm relations with their parents (Holmbeck, 1996), and children of all ages wish for more interaction time with parents. People are more busy at work, and work material is more accessible at home due to faxes, electronic mail, and voice mail. Therefore parents are less able to take free time just with the family. Since both parents often work, that leaves little quality time to spend with children overall. The current level of communication technology means also that it is pretty easy to keep up with people, so children may be able to use a cellular phone number or pager to get instant messages to a parent when necessary. At home, parents ought to ask their children about their day, their interests, and their feelings. The latter is critically important, as research has shown that children who have a strong emotional connection to their parents show fewer behavioral problems and attain higher academic achievements (Gottman, Katz, & Hooven, 1996).

Setting Appropriate Limits and Modifying Them as Children Age, Maintaining as Much Consistency as Possible

Consistency and reasoning are the most important ingredients in discipline. A lack of consistency tends to make discipline ineffective. Some parents will admonish a child for acting in an unacceptable way (such as screaming) at some times but not at others. What the child learns is that the behavior itself *is* acceptable, just not at certain times, such as in church. Other parents may choose to placate their children in public rather than to discipline them. Busy parents may not have the time to suspend an activity (such as shopping) to reason with a child. For example, a child fussing for some candy in the supermarket may be given the candy to quiet him, even if the parent does not want the child to have candy at that time. The child therefore learns to manipulate the parent under public circumstances in ways that would not work at home.

It is critical to set limits for children when they are young, since young children are often not capable of setting their own limits, and most are uncomfortable with too much freedom (Baumrind, 1980). Later when children are old enough to question, they can be allowed to take some responsibility for their own actions, that is, to co-regulate their behavior with the parent. Coregulation helps children develop a sense of themselves as competent. Self-competence is more rare in children of parents who are either very authoritarian or permissive (Baumrind, 1980).

Requiring Children to Expand Their Horizons While Providing Support for That Outreach

Children want opportunities to explore, but may hesitate, fearing negative outcomes. Parents must support children when they make mistakes, but not protect them so much that they never get a chance to become self-reliant. It may be beneficial to encourage children to seek goals, even if it is not clear they will succeed. By providing social support, parents can increase their children's willingness to try new experiences. Ainsworth's work on attachment suggested that this is true even in the first years of life (Ainsworth, 1983). Infants who could depend on their mothers to aid them when necessary treated their mothers as secure bases and were more likely to explore unfamiliar environments. Children whose parents use an authoritative parenting style will tend to be more inquisitive. Authoritarian parents' children do not try; they may have learned that behavior varying from their parents' expectations could lead to punishment. Permissive parents' children are protected from the consequences of their actions, so they do not learn much from their mistakes (Baumrind, 1980).

Teaching Them to Respect Laws and Authority, but to Act as Their Conscience Dictates–Modeling Moral Behavior to Help Them Develop Their Consciences

Prior to the 1960s when people started becoming more self-actualized, society conformed to fairly rigid social rules. Some of the social rules were based on customs (such as wearing gloves and hats to formal functions); others were rooted in traditional practices (such as mothers staying home with children rather than having careers). There were people who violated the rules, but they were seen as odd, unsophisticated, or even antisocial. Those who had little choice but to violate the rules (such as single mothers) were considered to belong on the fringes of society. Perhaps the distinction was appropriate at that time since there were so few working mothers. Economic and social changes in the past 30 years have greatly diminished adherence to rigid social rules. Now that nearly two-thirds of mothers of school-age children work outside the home, beliefs within the social system have also changed. Women who do *not* work outside the home (now in the minority) may be seen as socially radical (for choosing not to have a career when many others do so). To respond to changes in the social system, children need to have a solid base of family traditions and rituals or a strong internalization of family values to help them maintain a sense of coherence. These foundations often underlie a familial code of honor or morality.

Parents frequently do not discuss their own moral code with children, unless the children are violating that code. This makes it harder for the child to adopt the parents' rule system. Research suggests that adolescents learn about moral rules most effectively when they have examples of moral situations and solutions to those situations presented to them (Kohlberg, 1984). Parents who model moral behavior will have children who show moral behavior themselves, even when peers are engaging in antisocial behavior. Younger children will need the certainty of parental authority; adolescents will need the assurance that parents base actions on logical reasoning, so talking is crucial to developing children with solid moral reasoning. Parents may want to discuss differences between what the family wants and what society shows as acceptable behavior to gain what is desired. An important focus of parental instruction might be how, in the media (for example, television programs, books, and video games), violence is shown as a valid way to achieve goals. Parents can explain why that is not the best way to act.

WHAT ARE SOME WAYS TO START A FAMILY DIALOGUE AND TO KEEP IT GOING?

Creating Special Family Time

Parents need to start to make the family cohesive by setting aside family time when the CHILDREN ARE YOUNG–before they get involved in too many activities–and by making the time together fun and not allowing work or other responsibilities to pre-empt it. Setting up an expectation of family togetherness helps keep that togetherness going as family members' interests and lives diverge. Happy memories of childhood for close-knit families may include family get-to-gethers with the family, or even the extended family, for religious occasions, family birthdays, and even weekend visits. Children who grow up celebrating with the family come to value those interactions and will want to continue them as they get older.

Establishing Family Routines

One meaningful routine is to have a family dinner at least one night per week at which all family members are present and to permit no distraction from television or telephone. Even parents on a stressful career track NEED to put the family ahead of work or their own interests at times. Food and conversation also can lay the basis for other pleasant family interactions.

Whenever possible, parents should set aside a few days each month for family time, especially when weekend time is available. Family members could participate in board games or outdoor activities or watch a video together. In addition, if the family can volunteer together to help others, that is a good way to encourage children to realize that helping others is something that they should do. Some choices might be working with Habitat for Humanity, giving blood, or cleaning up a neighborhood park. To make the activity meaningful for all family members, the activity chosen should allow them all to participate in some way. Promoting family togetherness in a caring environment may help children to realize that helping others is important and also to reassure them that when they are in need, others may be there to help.

Emphasizing Family Togetherness over Individual Achievements

Curtail some individual nonessential activities or replace with those allowing some family members to be together–for example, if one of the daughters is on the basketball team, maybe her mother could spend a year coaching it, or if a son is interested in learning to play pool, maybe he and his father could learn together.

Making It a Priority for Family Members to Talk to Each Other

During family trips, discussions could be encouraged instead of listening to the radio or reading. The discussions could involve family issues and should include all children able to engage in the conversation. For example, if a mother is considering having another child, she might ask the children how they feel about that possibility. That type of interaction also encourages children to talk to their parents when making decisions of their own, perhaps later when a child is concerned about drugs, academic problems, or sexuality. One way to encourage a child to treat parents as confidantes is for the parents to treat that child as a confidante.

Sometimes parents wait with one child to pick up another child from some activity. Having some individual time alone with a parent is special to a child. Some parents plan to spend time with one child doing something that child likes or maybe just sharing new experiences with the child. This may be especially important if the family has more than two children or if a child feels less appreciated than a sibling.

Explaining Parents' Views on Social Issues

Parents need to discuss social issues that they feel are important with their children, for example, racism or school prayer. If parents are uncomfortable bringing up certain issues, such as sexuality, they might sit with the child to watch a video or television program that deals with the issue (for example, teen violence can be discussed while or after watching a movie with inter-teen violence).

Recognizing When Children Need Assistance and Providing It

Children send parents a variety of signals, including clear warnings, but parents are not always attentive to these. People were shocked that parents of the teens who killed schoolmates in Columbine were un-aware of their teens' plans, but parents often fail to keep in touch with their teens due to a belief that the teen is more adult-like and not in need of supervision. Limit-setting is still important, although parents should take advantage of coregulation as children age, and teens can participate in setting appropriate limits for themselves.

Being Aware of Children's Activities

Taking advantage of safeguards such as the v-chip or software programs that screen undesirable web sites can help parents, but they must not let those be the only way they cope with potential problems for their child. It is crucial to be aware of which activities children are engaged in. Although some children (especially adolescents) may ex-press dissatisfaction with being scrutinized, they are often actually happy that their parents are concerned about them.

Maintaining Family Ties

Finally, keeping in close contact with the extended family by visiting or at least by telephone is important. With electronic mail increasingly available, it is easier than ever to keep in correspondence. Currently, many companies offer free electronic mail accounts. If grandparents do not have a computer, parents may consider going in with other family members to buy one and having a family member teach the grandparents how to use it.

Maintaining close spousal relations is an important component in raising a family. Active, attentive parenting is another critical factor. Practices that encourage children to be insightful about their behavior and their environment will help children develop good social perception skills. Lastly, parents and children must communicate well and often. If families try to follow these steps, they can achieve warm, productive relationships.

REFERENCES

Ainsworth, M.D.S. (1983). Patterns of infant-mother attachment as related to maternal care. In D. Magnusson & V. Allen (Eds.), *Human development: An interactional perspective*. New York: Academic Press.

Anderson, S.A., Russell, C.S., & Schumm, W.R. (1983). Perceived marital quality and family-life cycle categories: A further analysis. *Journal of Marriage and the Family, 45*, 227-239.

Arditti, J.A. (1992). Differences between fathers with joint custody and noncustodial fathers. *American Journal of Orthopsychiatry, 62*, 186-195.

Bandura, A. (1989). Social cognitive theory. In R. Vasta (Ed.), *Annals of Child Development*, (Vol. 6, pp. 1-60). Greenwich, CT: JAI Press.

Baumrind, D. (1980). New directions in socialization research. *American Psychologist, 35*, 639-652.

Beck, R.W. & Beck, S.W. (1989). The incidence of extended households among middle-aged black and white women. *Journal of Family Issues, 10*, 147-168.

Belsky, J., Youngblade, L., Rovine, M, and Volling, B. (1991). Patterns of marital change and parent-child interaction. *Journal of Marriage and the Family, 53*, 487-498.

Gottman, J.M., Katz, L.F., & Hooven, C. (1996). Parental meta-emotion philosophy and the emotional lives of families: Theoretical models and preliminary data. *Journal of Family Psychology, 10*, 243-268.

Gray, J. (1992). *Men are from Mars, women are from Venus*. New York: HarperCollins.

Harrison, A.O., Wilson, M.N., Pine, C.J., Can, S.Q., & Buriel, R. (1994). Family ecologies of ethnic minority children. In G. Handel & G.G. Whitchurch (Eds.), *The psychological interior of the family* (pp. 187-210). New York: Aldine de Gruyter.

Kohlberg, L. (1984). *Essays on moral development, Volume 2. The psychology of moral development.* New York: Harper and Row.

Ludwig, D.J. (2000). It's the relationship, stupid! *Journal of Family Social Work* 4(3), 1-30.

Piotrkowski, C.S. & Hughes, D. (1993). Dual-earner families in context: Managing family and work systems. In F. Walsh (Ed.), *Normal family processes* (2nd ed.), (pp. 185-207). New York: Guilford.

Spock, B. & Rothenberg, M.B. (1992). *Dr. Spock's baby and child care.* New York: Pocket Books.

Stanley, S.M., Markman, H.J., St. Peters, M., & Leber, B.D. (1995). Strengthening marriages and preventing divorce: New direction in prevention research. *Family Relations: Journal of Applied Family and Child Studies, 44,* 392-401.

Young, P. (1991). Parents with adolescents. In F.H. Brown (Ed.), *Reweaving the family tapestry* (pp. 131-168). New York: Norton.

The Family Unit:
PLACE, BASE or Both?

William B. Knippa, PhD, MDiv

SUMMARY. It is obvious that there are a variety of family structures and forms. This variety is usually described in terms of the nature of the parental presence, namely, two parent, single-parent, and step-parent (or blended) families. There is also variety regarding life stages, usually described in terms of the presence or absence of children with a focus on their age; e.g., families with infants, toddlers, elementary age children, adolescents, or "empty nesters." But in what ways does the core purpose of the family in the lives of its members remain constant regardless of the family's configuration or life stage? How might this constancy impact the task of those who deal with families from both theoretical and therapeutic perspectives? This paper addresses these questions by presenting a simply-stated framework defining the purpose of the family that focuses on the nature of an individual's *relationship* to his or her family regardless of that family's life stage or structure. The breakdown of the "WE" of the family unit as the source of family pathology and dysfunction will be described within this framework and therapeutic strategies presented. *[Article copies available for a fee from The Haworth Document Delivery Service: 1-800-342-9678. E-mail address: <getinfo@haworthpressinc.com> Website: <http://www.haworthpressinc.com>]*

KEYWORDS. Family structure, family life stages, family dysfunction, network of relationships, "PLACE" problems, "BASE" problems, marital bond ("WE"), unconditional love, genograms

The core purpose of the family is to create and sustain a *network of relationships* that provide its members a PLACE in which one "grows" and BASE from which one "goes." This simple statement is

---

William B. Knippa is a Licensed Psychologist and also Pastor of Bethany Lutheran Church, Austin, TX.

[Haworth co-indexing entry note]: "The Family Unit: PLACE, BASE or Both?" Knippa, William B. Co-published simultaneously in *Journal of Family Social Work* (The Haworth Press, Inc.) Vol. 4, No. 3, 2000, pp. 51-63; and: *Social Work and the Family Unit* (ed: David J. Ludwig) The Haworth Press, Inc., 2000, pp. 51-63. Single or multiple copies of this article are available for a fee from The Haworth Document Delivery Service [1-800-342-9678, 9:00 a.m. - 5:00 p.m. (EST). E-mail address: getinfo@haworthpressinc.com].

not meant to deny the complexity of a family system. Indeed, the theoretical approaches to family therapy as represented by different schools introduced in the last generation, such as conjoint (Satir, 1964), structural (Minuchin, 1974), systemic (Bowen, 1978), strategic (Madanes, 1981), symbolic-experiential (Whitaker, 1988), object relations (Scharff & Scharff, 1991) and others (Gurman, 1981), speak to the complexity of family systems. Families are intricate, dynamic organisms. Rather, it is hoped that the simple picture of a family as a PLACE and a BASE will provide an organizing template that will be helpful when working with families regardless of one's theoretical approach.

UNDERSTANDING PLACE AND BASE

Providing a PLACE speaks to an individual's need for connection, closeness, and community. Having a PLACE is associated with security and the experience of "less" as opposed to "more" anxiety in an individual's life. The family, except in rare instances, is the relational context within which PLACE is first desired, expected and sought. Difficulties arise when an individual in a family does not experience having a PLACE of physical and emotional security in which growth can optimally occur.

Providing a BASE speaks to an individual's need to have a foundation from which to launch into the world and thus separate from the family. Ideally, when an individual has experienced a "good enough" PLACE, he or she will then move out of the family of origin into the larger world of individuality, responsibility, and maturity. Difficulties arise when the relationships, especially the "WE" between the parents (Ludwig, 1997), are not healthy. The individual is then not able or allowed to "launch" from the home BASE and thus remains fused with family.

The importance of family relationships as a source of an individual's sense of PLACE continues as one moves through the life cycle. During one's formative years in the parental household, the sense of PLACE is reinforced through daily and frequent contact with family members. The relational quality of these contacts creates the relational and hence the emotional atmosphere which the child breathes (Ludwig, 1989). Assuming the PLACE is providing adequately clean and fresh air, a toddler is able to begin exploring her world. A child is able to establish himself in school, make friends, begin to develop unique aspects of his personality, become more social, and begin equipping himself for life separate from direct parental control.

Very early in an individual's life, then, the PLACE for growing becomes a BASE for going into the world. Depending on one's experience, she or he associates a given level of security and strength with the sense of family as PLACE. As one moves from this environment into the world at large, one continues to go back in one's mind to the family PLACE. When that PLACE houses memories, pictures, and thoughts that are warm and strengthening, one is energized to face the challenges of the relationships and life tasks of the present. When one goes back to the family PLACE and finds oneself alone or distressed, the present is negatively impacted. For instance, the thirty-five-year-old daughter who calls home to "touch base" with mom or dad is, in some way, desiring to connect to a source of security, to experience again that she has a PLACE in their hearts and mind. The twenty-eight-year-old son who keeps volunteering information about his work to his father, even though his father continually fails to take any interest, is still seeking a deepened sense of PLACE in his father's life. The sixty-five-year-old man who still wonders why his mother never, ever said she loved him while having no problem saying it to his two siblings is still looking for a PLACE.

Should the thirty-five, twenty-eight and sixty-year-old adults be able to "get on" with their lives without encouragement or empowerment from parents? Well, yes. But, if family members can be encouraged and equipped to see their continued importance in one another's lives in providing a PLACE for emotional connection and a BASE from which one is effectively launched and re-launched into the world, their *relationship* with one another will be a blessing and not a curse. This is a worthy goal for families and for those who have invested considerable time, training, and energy in becoming competent in assisting families to function in healthful ways.

THERAPEUTIC IMPLICATIONS

One approach, then, to working with families is to discern to what degree a family is providing a secure PLACE for its members and to what degree it is serving as an empowering BASE from which its members individuate. The symptoms manifesting in a given family may have their roots as a PLACE problem, a BASE problem, or a combination of both. The nature of the problem will drive the direction of the treatment.

So, when a family comes seeking help, the therapist can discern whether the major presenting issue, regardless on whom it is centering in the family is a PLACE or BASE problem. Is the distress the family is experiencing a function of a member or members not experiencing a secure connection? Is it a PLACE problem? Or, is the distress primarily a function of a lack of individuation in certain family members? Is it a BASE problem?

PLACE problems include:

- marital discord related to a spouse's feeling isolated, distanced, unappreciated and the behaviors chosen in reaction to these feelings
- the presence of physical, emotional or sexual abuse
- poor conflict resolution skills
- ineffective ways of dealing with anger
- rigid and inflexible family rules, implicit or explicit, which are deemed more important than the people and relationships in the family
- acting out
- school failure
- truancy or other legal problems
- inability for family members to talk about matters of personal or mutual importance
- sexual promiscuity and other risk taking behaviors by family members

PLACE problems have at their root: a family member(s):

- being exposed to physical threat, danger, or abuse
- experiencing a sense of being devalued and thus not connected
- failing to be acknowledged as a individual in one's own right

BASE problems include:

- marital discord related to a spouse's being overly invested in one's family of origin to the detriment of the present family
- social anxieties and phobias which keep a family member confined within the family

- difficulty with or refusal to accept new members into the family via marriage
- an adult child returning home and being reluctant to leave due to dependency needs
- over-control of a child by a parent
- emotional or physical punishment of a family member because of his or her taking steps that express independence and responsibility for one's thoughts and actions

BASE problems have at their root:

- a poor marital bond that demands a child remain triangled in PLACE in order to meet needs of one or both parents and thus reduce their anxiety
- a spouse remaining triangled in his or her family of origin
- residual anxiety in a parent or parents stemming from that parent(s) not having experienced a secure PLACE in his or her family of origin
- family patterns infected with fear, depression, or abuse

When facing a PLACE problem, the task is to work with the family in order to assist in bringing them closer together. When facing a BASE problem, the task is to work with the family in order to assist them in being able to be separate from one another and engaged in the world.

THE IMPORTANCE OF THE MARITAL BOND ("WE") AS PLACE AND BASE

After assessing the source of the problem, the next step is to determine the strengths and weaknesses in the marriage bond, again looking at the marriage from the perspective of PLACE and BASE. How strong is each spouse's sense of physical and emotional security, of PLACE? Do they know how to be close? Or, to what degree has each been able to establish a sense of individuality and comfort with the other's separateness? Have they learned how to respect the other as a separate person so that the marriage serves as a good BASE that empowers each to live in the world? Therapists have available a wide variety of approaches and techniques to utilize in working with couples and should employ those they deem most helpful in assisting a couple in knowing how to be close and how to be separate–how to provide a PLACE and a BASE for one another in marriage. In the case of a single parent, the question to be asked is how that parent is meeting his or her needs to have a sense of PLACE, of being connected, close, and in community. The initial focus of treatment would involve assisting the parent in establishing a sense of PLACE in the adult world and within the context of adult relationships, separate from the child, as well as working to empower the parent to create as secure a place for the child. If the single parent has very little sense of PLACE, and if that parent expects the child(ren) to meet that need, the child will be overloaded. He or she will be expected to provide a PLACE instead of enjoying a PLACE that should be provided by the parent.

THE FAMILY AS SECURE PLACE

Broadly speaking, a family provides a secure PLACE for its members when:

- the parents form a "WE"
- the family is free of physical threat and abuse of any kind
- its members experience a sense of being valued
- its members are acknowledged as individuals in their own right
- there is a sense of shared history which links them together in time and space

PLACE AND PHYSICAL SAFETY

When a therapist encounters a family in which physical threats, danger, and abuse are present, decisive and direct action must be taken. The legal and social mechanisms available to deal with these issues are in place in most communities and familiar to most helpers. Consequently, it is not necessary to explore or enumerate treatment options. Those are known. Suffice it to say that such a family environment seriously erodes or completely destroys that family's credibility as a secure PLACE. Thus its members' anxiety is raised, safety is denied, and its level of functioning plummets.

PLACE AND THE IMPORTANCE OF BEING VALUED IN THE FAMILY

Classic attachment literature and research (Bolby, 1969) describes the vital importance of a developing individual being connected to a source of warmth and nurturance. It is as if each newborn child has an emotional battery that must be charged in order for him or her to thrive. The battery is charged when the child experiences his or her basic needs being met within the context of a warm, close relationship. Physical touch, eye contact, response to food and elimination urges, and warm attention meet the child's basic survival needs and are experienced as both soothing and empowering. It is as if the child says,

> I matter. I am worthy of being tuned into and noticed by the person whose power makes it possible for me to exist. As long I am thus noticed and acknowledged, I will survive. If, for some reason, I become no longer valuable enough to this person to merit her attention and action, I will be abandoned. I will cease to exist. I won't make it.

What the child needs, and what the older individual seeks, is a sense that,

> I will continue to be valued by that person or persons to whom I have given power in my life, regardless of my behavior, attitude, or appearance.

To experience this is to experience unconditional love or unconditional positive regard, and with it a sense of being valued. When a family member senses and believes that she is valued on the basis of who she is and not on the basis of what she does or doesn't do or accomplish, the bond to family is strengthened and emotional security is enhanced. While a great deal of love is present in most every family, the delivery system can be flawed. A family member can be loved and valued but not feel it. When dealing with relationships, the emotions are vital. Hence, if someone doesn't feel valued, he will assume, in general, that he is not. Some ways in which the delivery system can be flawed are through:

- marital conflict that drains the amount of emotional energy and attention available to the child and focuses it in another direction
- parent(s) assuming that a child should "know" he or she is loved without expressing it through eye contact, appropriate physical contact, and focused attention
- the presence of an alcoholic or "rageaholic" parent

- verbally abusive language in the family
- parental narcissism
- difficulty expressing emotions in the family
- failure to have the desire or mechanisms in place to forgive family hurts, betrayals or transgressions or deal with resentments, bitterness, and jealousy

The presence of these factors drain the emotional battery of a family member, increase anxiety in the system, and manifest as dysfunction.

As an individual moves into adulthood, knowing he or she is valued by both nuclear and extended family members continues to be a source of emotional connection and security as well as a source of strength to continue to activate oneself in the world.

In order to determine family members' perception of how valued each is in the family, they can be asked to indicate such on a ten point scale. There is the overall sense of "My family" as well as the breaking down of family into individual members; i.e., Dad is about a "9" on loving me no matter what. Mom is a "3." An answer like this may indicate some problems between dad and mom that are focused on the child.

My family loves me "no matter what"

0 10

Never true   Always true

The responses can open doors of communication on this most important facet of family life. Thoughtful analysis by the therapist as to the source of the responses and appropriate ways to assist family members in connecting is essential. The focus is "Who isn't feeling valued, and by whom?" "Why?" "What resources does the family possess that can be activated in order for their connection to be enhanced?" "Where is the delivery system breaking down?"

PLACE AND THE IMPORTANCE OF BEING AFFIRMED AS A UNIQUE INDIVIDUAL

While people can be grouped and categorized on any number of variables, the fact remains that individual differences abound. Every person possesses a uniqueness that distinguishes him or her from every other individual. The family is the arena in which such uniqueness can be acknowledged, affirmed, and encouraged. As an individual in the family experiences this, his or her emotional battery is charged and the sense of the family being a secure PLACE is enhanced. Distress in this area of family life stems from a number of sources. One is the need that some parents have to shape their child in their own image or to live vicariously through their child. The child's unique attributes, gifts, interests, and talents are ignored. The influence of birth order, temperament, and life experience is discounted. There are also situations in which a child's physical features and idiosyncrasies stir up unpleasant associations in a parent's mind. The child is then subject to being punished in some way on the basis of intrinsic qualities over which she has no control. In addition, a parent can be threatened because a child is more talented or able in certain areas of life. Again, the child is discouraged from developing or demonstrating those qualities.

Most therapists have experienced encountering families in which one child is constantly being compared to another. For example, an active and kinesthetically gifted child is expected to be calm and cerebral; an introverted child is expected to be extroverted; a musically gifted child is told, she "shouldn't be wasting her time on that kind of stuff"; or one spouse is trying to change the other to more nearly conform to perfection. Attempts by forces in the family to form its members like plastic into a fixed mold can and often does continue regardless of their ages. It creates distress in the fifty-year-old as well as the five-year-old. At times, what one would expect in a family is reversed in that a child doesn't accept the uniqueness of a parent. The child wants his mother to be more attractive, a son wants his father to quit a job he loves to take one that pays more, an adult woman won't introduce her mother to her business partner because the daughter judges her mother to have poor taste in clothes. Regardless of where the lack of affirmation of uniqueness is rooted, it undermines the sense of family as a relationally secure and safe PLACE. Asking family members to respond to the following question on a ten-point scale can be instructive in discerning how family members perceive themselves being accepted by other family members. Again, breaking down responses on the basis of individual family members as well as the family as a whole can be instructive in looking at the different relational networks that exist in a family.

My family accepts me for who I am

0 10

Never true   Always true

The therapist can take this information and use it to assist family members in understanding how other family members perceive themselves on this important dimension. Also, conversation can be facilitated which allows those who believe their uniqueness, and thus a crucial part of themselves, has been denied an opportunity to be heard. Being heard, and having that acknowledged by those to whom one has granted considerable importance, is empowering. In addition, this information can assist family members in acknowledging and affirming the uniqueness of each family member. This in turn contributes to strengthening the family a PLACE to grow and have one's emotional battery charged.

PLACE AND FAMILY HISTORY

A sense of having a secure PLACE is enhanced when members have a sense that they are a part of something larger than themselves, that larger something being the relationship network that existed in the past, is present at the moment, and will unfold into the future. One means of reestablishing and reinforcing this is for family members to have knowledge of its history, its roots. From where did we come? What was life like for those in our family two and three generations past? What kind of vocations and skills were employed? What were the family's significant failures and successes? Who were its prominent personages, both heroes and villains. How have these and other past factors and influences shaped the family's physical, emotional, spiritual, and material world. Woven into the family's past history are the traditions, practices, events, and rituals of the present as well as the hopes and dreams of the future. These combine to strengthen the fabric of the family and give it a continuity in time and space that deepens the experience of family as a secure PLACE. When family history is freely shared there may well be a decrease in family secrets which, when otherwise present, work to balkanize the family into separate subgroups and lay land mines that often explode on the uninformed. Completing a genogram (McGoldrick, 1985) with the family is one way to see how much family history is known and shared. Another way would be to have family members rate on a one to ten scale how informed each is on the history of the last three generations. Including young children in this exercise is not very helpful. However, teenagers often are curious about or actually know more family history than might be expected.

How much do you know about your family's history of the last three generations?

0 10

Nothing at all   A great deal

This would serve as a discussion starter and be diagnostic as well. Ignorance of family history could indicate persistent generational secrets, trauma or crises that were too distressing to share, a pattern of emotional "cut off's," pronounced problems with parents and grandparents, or similar dysfunction. Addressing generational issues under the guidance of a competent therapist can be of great benefit. When emotional arteries connected to the previous generation are cleared, more emotional energy can flow into the present and succeeding generation, helping to create a PLACE that extends itself in time.

THE FAMILY AS BASE

When the family has functioned as a secure PLACE for its members to be connected and to grow, it has usually provided a strong BASE for launching as well. When PLACE has been chaotic or hostile to the individual, difficulties often arise in the way a person then relates to the family of origin. Some individuals leave the family as soon as possible and set out on their own. Others leave in frustration but return often hoping to experience family as a PLACE of security. "Maybe this time dad will tell me he's proud of me" or "Maybe mom won't drink too much this Thanksgiving." But things don't usually change simply because someone wants them to change. Some family members, sucked into the vortex of family dysfunction, never leave, never establish themselves as separate individuals, and never develop their gifts or abilities.

When a family presents with a BASE problem, a problem centering on difficulties in family members separating from one another, first look to see in what kind of PLACE the family is and what it is providing its members. Respond accordingly. If this appears to be "good enough," look at the relationship that exists or existed between the present and past parental generation. A parent who has difficulty "letting go" of a child appropriately is often still working through personal issues that have caused him or her to attach to a child or spouse in such a way as to meet needs for being valued, loved, connected that should have been met in their family of origin PLACE. As a way of broaching the issue to being separate while still a member of a family, ask the parent(s) to respond to the following:

I have been able to exercise independence in relation to my parents

0 10

Never true   Always true

As discussion and therapeutic intent continues, assist the family in understanding and in experiencing that their connection–their PLACE in one another's lives–is a function of valuing one another and communicating that value, acknowledging, affirming and encouraging one another's uniqueness, and sharing a common history, These experiences can continue regardless of physical or visual proximity and serve to charge one another's emotional batteries.

CONCLUSION

Family relationships exert considerable power on its members throughout their lives. This power can be a source of encouragement or discouragement, of delight or despair, of strength or weakness. Regardless of an individual's age, the family can provide a PLACE of emotional security. This is true for the infant who will fail to thrive without it. This is true for the college student who knows he can call home after bombing a test and still get a good and warm word from his parents. This is true for the newly widowed woman whose children encompass her with support. Each knows, on a level appropriate to their age and circumstance, that family is a PLACE of value, affirmation, and connection. The family also serves as a need BASE from which one launches into the world. The child who attends kindergarten with excitement, the young adult who takes on a challenging course of studies, job assignment or family responsibilities, and the octogenarian who has been given six hours to live and is surrounded by his loved ones know that family has provided a BASE from which one can take the next step of one's journey.

Understanding the importance of healthy family relationships and using the template of family as a PLACE and BASE can focus the therapist's energy and thought on two aspects of family life that are crucial to family health in a way that can be simply understood. Utilization of therapeutic skills, insights and experiences can assist family members in experiencing their relationships and connections as providing a secure PLACE for growing throughout the life cycle. Therapists are also in a position to assist a family in becoming an empowering BASE from which its members go into the world to use their gifts, develop their potential, contribute to the common good, and thus provide a PLACE and a BASE for the next generation.

REFERENCES

Bolby, J. (1969). *Attachment and Loss* (Vol. 1). New York: Basic Books.

Bowen, M. (1978). *Family Therapy in Clinical Practice*. New York: Jason Aronson.

Gurman, S. and Kniskern, D., Eds. (1981). *Handbook of Family Therapy*. New York: Brunner/Mazel.

Ludwig, D. (1989). *Renewing the Family Spirit* (Book and Video). St. Louis: Concordia Publishing House.

Ludwig, D. (1997). *The Power of WE* (Book and Video). St. Louis: Concordia Publishing House.

McGoldrick, M. & Gerson, R. (1985). *Genograms in Family Assessment*. New York: W.W. Norton.

Madanes. C. (1981). *Strategic Family Therapy*. San Franciso: Jossey-Bass.

Minuchin, S. (1974). *Families and Family Therapy*. Cambridge, MA: Harvard University Press.

Satir, V. (1964). *Conjoint Family Therapy*. Palo Alto: Science and Behavior Books, Inc.

Scharff, D. & Scharff, J. (1991). *Object Relations Family Therapy*. Northvale, N.J., Jason Aronson.

Whiteaker, C. & Bumberry, W. (1980). *Dancing With the Family: A Symbolic-Experiential Approach*. New York: Brunner/Mazel.

The Relational Systems Model:
Reality and Self-Differentiation

Donald R. Bardill, PhD

SUMMARY. This article addresses two of the major theoretical considerations that undergird the Relational Systems Model for Family Therapy. The concept of life realities posits that all that exists in the realm of human *relationships* may be viewed as a circle of reality consisting of self, other, context, and spiritual. Inviting clients to connect with these realities rather than human-created versions helps clients bring into awareness vital information that is actually present, but not manifest in the clients' problem-saturated lives. The self-differentiation process for the therapist is proposed as the therapeutic energy that enables clients to expand their awareness of vital parts of reality. *[Article copies available for a fee from The Haworth Document Delivery Service: 1-800-342-9678. E-mail address: <getinfo@haworthpressinc.com> Website: <http://www.haworthpressinc.com>]*

KEYWORDS. Relational Systems Model (RSM), life realities, self-differentiation, self-reality, context, social constructionist, spiritual reality, self-regulation, self-definition

The application of Relational Systems Model (RSM) largely rests on the therapist's ability to utilize the clinical implications inherent in the concepts of life realities and self-differentiation. First, the concept of life realities posits that all that exists in the realm of human relationships may be viewed within a circle-of-reality that includes three human realities–self, other, and context–and a fourth reality, the spiri-

---

Donald R. Bardill is Professor, School of Social Work, Florida State University, Tallahassee, FL.

[Haworth co-indexing entry note]: "The Relational Systems Model: Reality and Self-Differentiation." Bardill, Donald R. Co-published simultaneously in *Journal of Family Social Work* (The Haworth Press, Inc.) Vol. 4, No. 3, 2000, pp. 65-77; and: *Social Work and the Family Unit* (ed: David J. Ludwig) The Haworth Press, Inc., 2000, pp. 65-77. Single or multiple copies of this article are available for a fee from The Haworth Document Delivery Service [1-800-342-9678, 9:00 a.m. - 5:00 p.m. (EST). E-mail address: getinfo@haworthpressinc.com].

tual. Second, the dynamics of self-differentiation are regarded as pivotal to the process of psychotherapy because of their importance both to the clinician and the client. The primary purpose of this paper is to examine the clinical implications that evolve from an examination and integration of RSM life realities and self-differentiation dynamics.

It may be noted that, philosophically, RSM embraces much of the fallibilistic thinking of Karl Popper. Humans, as finite beings, are limited in the extent of their perceptual capacities. Thus, we see only part of "what is," of reality. Through certain life processes, which include effective psychotherapy, humans are able to expand their awareness of certain realities. Indeed, one of the fundamental purposes of the RSM form of psychotherapy is to bring forth for clients that which is present but not yet manifest in their lives.

THE REALITIES

In RSM, reality is defined as "what is." For purposes of our discussion, imagine that all of reality is contained in a circle-of-reality. Within this circle-of-reality are four realities that are experientially available to human beings. (See below.)

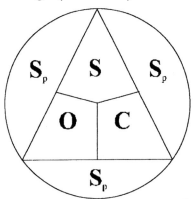

The makeup of our human sensory system defines what we can experience. For instance, we have internal nerve receptors that give us a subjective sense of ourselves. We have sensory receptors that allow us to experience animate and inanimate objects outside ourselves. We have a brain that enables us to experience the meaning of the physical and social environment in which we live. We evolve an awareness that we are part of something larger than ourselves. Given our human capacities we are able to experience realities this author shall call self, other, context, and the spiritual.

SELF

I can experience that I exist. I not only experience my existence, I experience my experiences. I have self-awareness. Self may be called reality in the subjective sense. I simply know that I exist. I know that I am "what is" because of my innate capacities to do such things as think, feel, be self-aware, form mental images, remember, create ideas, set priorities, and make meaning. Yet, one's real-self or self (self and real-self may be used interchangeably) is not easy to comprehend. Out of the real-self evolves a personal context or position from which one views one's own life. In other words, each of us creates our own individual world-view.

Self may be regarded as the source of all of my personal identities, labels, and images. Although self is the source of all my identities, it is not one of them. An awareness of the distinction between the real-self and the self's many personal creations is vital to the human maturity process.

> In the RSM, it is important to understand that the self is not a belief, it is not a value or ideology that you hold, though is a *part* of a larger view toward life that you hold. Humans get attached and committed to certain values, beliefs, ideologies, and traditions. We begin to think that we *are* our views and rigidly defend them. The point is not to lack views. The point is not to get rigidly stuck in specific, narrow human perspectives. To be stuck in such a position is to be unable to assume other viewpoints, to lose creativity, or to be locked in narrow thinking. Again, and very important, self is more than any value, belief, ideology, tradition, role, etc. The well-differentiated self has the function of not getting locked into one of the above in such a way as to regard any one of them as the self. If a value, belief, role, etc., is regarded as self we defend it on a survival basis. It is the self that has the task of not allowing the mind to be taken *over* by emotions, feelings, or thinking *and* at the same time allowing for the expression of emotions, feelings, and thinking. Self is the personal context for all that I am.

The self is dependent upon the functioning of the brain yet it clearly is more than the genetic instructions that run the brain. I am more than my genetic coding, my social experiences, and my education. We are self-differentiated beings to the extent that (1) we can know our positions, viewpoints, contexts, and internal demands, *and* we can transcend them; (2) we can assume various viewpoints, and be creative, open to other viewpoints, and not be stuck or frozen in a position; *AND*–a very big AND–(3) know who and what we are from considerations of love, caring, and integrity. The self is the major player in my life. I am real! It is a reality! (Bardill, 1997)

All humans have the life-long task of maintaining a distinction between the real-self and the personal items and identities which the real-self creates. For example, take a moment to give attention to your most strongly held identity. It may be race, gender, work role, family role, etc. Next, write a brief letter to that created-identity. One woman chose her "nice person" identity. From the point of view of an observer she told the "nice person" what that created part of her meant to her. The woman talked about both the positives and negatives that are associated with living the "nice person" identity.

The letter provided the woman an enhanced awareness about a strong governing part of her. This brief exercise allowed her to experience a created item that is connected to her real-self but is not her real self. Other useful exercises include writing a poem to an identity that is created by the real-self. All of us have many created items that are connected to our real-selves but are not our real-selves.

Self-reality raises two important points in RSM thinking. First, one of the purposes of psychotherapy is to make known that which is present but not yet manifest. Conscious attention to the distinction between the reality of the self and the creations of the real-self brings forth an enhanced present reality. Second, it is well to remember that that which we create we may uncreate. We may choose to give up or alter any one of our strongly held but personally created items.

OTHER

The "other-reality" may be defined as everything that is, organic and inorganic. While all aspects of the other-reality are important, of special attention for RSM is other people. I experience other people. Other people experience me and communicate about their experiences of me. We are connected to other people in different and complex ways. The parent-child connection, the sibling connection, the family connection, the husband-wife and peer connections are just a few of the most apparent forms of relationships with the other reality.

The very continuation and growth of the human race is founded on the intimacy of commitment of an adult male and an adult female to each other and to the care of their children (Bardill, 1998). Indeed, a measure of human emotional maturity is the ability to maintain a distinct self within an intimate committed relationship with one's spouse.

Much like the distinction between the real-self and the personal items created by the real-self there is a vital difference between the reality of another person and our created images/pictures of that person. We humans bring images of persons from the past into our present relationships with other people. Based on past images and past relationships with another we create internalized images of a particular person in the present. In all human relationships a fundamental question is this: To what degree am I relating to my created/remembered image of an individual rather than the actual other? Human beings have a strong tendency to treat other people as if they were not distinct realities. Thus, we are inclined to view another person as an extension of ourselves. When we do not experience others as distinct realities we relate to them as a created-other, a creation of our real-self.

Troubled relationships almost always involve a high degree of created-other transactions by one or more participants. Virginia Satir found "at least 90 percent of any difficulty between two people had to do with their pictures and assumptions of each other rather than connecting with each other" (Satir et al., 1991). For a compelling exercise that demonstrates the importance of the distinction between the created-other and the actual other read the exercise "With whom am I having the pleasure" in Satir et al., 1991.

In engaging the reality of other people it is impossible not to create images/pictures of others. The fact of created-others is not the problem. Indeed, our ability to empathize with others comes from our capacity to picture an event from another person's perspective. The accuracy with which we "walk a mile in another's moccasins" enables us to understand another person. Troubles in accounting for other people most often emerge when we lose our awareness of the extent to which we are relating to the created-other rather than the actual other.

A powerful exercise for connecting with the essence of a child is provided in the chapter "Positive Parenting" in Connerae and Andreas's book *Heart of the Mind* (1989). In summary, the parent is invited to find a comfortable quiet place to engage in an imaginal process which includes these steps. (1) Think of a difficult situation with your child, one that happens frequently. (2) Reexperience the difficult episode from your point of view. You may do this several times. (3) Visualize this same experience but from the viewpoint of your child. Take a moment to become your child, notice any new information, allow yourself to be your child. You may repeat the episode from start to finish several times. (4) Experience the same situation but this time as an observer. What do you see? (5) Make use of the new information. Allow yourself to see and learn new information. Use your inner wisdom!

CONTEXT

Context, the third reality in our circle, is that which exists in the objective sense. Humans have the capacity to experience and make meaning of the social environment into which they are born and into which they are socialized.

> We come into the world with a predetermined set of social contexts. Our context is laid upon us through such entities as government, bureaucracy, culture, religion, communities, families, and other institutions created by people. These people-created contexts have been handed down from generation to generation. The content of the context-reality is a learned reality. Humankind learns about values, expectations, beliefs, and morals through the socialization process. All societies, primitive and sophisticated, have contextual factors which serve to regulate and define behavior. (Bardill, 1997)

In every sense, the context is a socially constructed reality. Humans make up their own social context. It is that part of our existence that comes from the patterns, structures, and transactions of life. It may be thought of as the prepackaged thoughts of society, culture, etc. Context is a made-up reality that serves as our frame of reference for making meaning of events. In one context a word may have one meaning; in another context the same word may have another meaning. For instance, the word *ring* has one meaning in a wedding ceremony and another one with reference to the noise a phone makes.

The thinking of the social constructionists primarily addresses context-reality. Social constructionist theory recognizes the finiteness of human beings and of their connection to a limited part of reality and then only from a narrow perspective. Social constructionist theory holds that our beliefs about the world are social inventions (Hoffman, 1990). Over time we have used communication to establish an ecology-of-ideas (a social invention) that we use as our map of the world. Social constructionist theory distinguishes that the map is only a map; it is *not* the territory itself. RSM by its nature invites clients to give attention to the distinctions among the various powerful social constructions that govern our lives.

There are vital pieces of information about context-reality that are important to RSM. First, context-reality is a created reality. Context consists of the stories society or any social system tells itself in order to make sense of the world. Thus, we use context to make meaning and, therefore, to survive. Context-reality continually is being formed out of the communicated ideas of collectives of people. Second, context is a powerful reality that cannot be ignored. Third, context is an outworking, a product, of human nature. Fourth, the nature and content of context changes over time thereby requiring that we constantly update. Social difficulties and societal regression are likely when we lose or lack awareness of the constructed quality of our social context. Fifth, humans perceive life through a glass darkly, i.e., we see only a narrow view of "what is." Sixth, that which is humanly constructed may be deconstructed. We have the capacity to change our context.

Take a moment to reflect on some strongly held ideas that have been passed along to you from such a context as your family, your community, your profession, your race, your gender, your religion, your country, etc. Select one context-created item and think about the ideas, values, beliefs, and stories contained within that item that have influenced you over the years. What particular notions have been useful, not very useful, or harmful to you? How strongly attached are you to any particular idea? Are you aware that all the items that make up a context have been created by humans as part of our efforts to survive and to grow? We live in a created world. We can re-create our context.

The distinction between our image of the world and what is actually out there opens an empowering pathway to change. Knowing that we all have images of the world makes us realize that whatever image we have is likely to be inaccurate and distorted in some way. At the same time, since images can be changed much more easily than the world, this knowledge also provides us with the freedom and ability to see things differently. (Andreas, 1991)

Most current narrative therapies and solution-oriented therapies employ some form of constructionist theory that informs us about clients and the therapeutic procedures that will enable them to work on solutions to their perceived problems (White & Epston, 1990; Eron & Lund, 1996). An important goal of narrative thinking is to help people tell their stories, reflect upon their stories, and incorporate solution-saturated content into their stories. The social constructionist perspective has provided great advances in the task of addressing context-reality with our clients.

Given the created nature of much that takes place within people as well as between and among people, clients are invited, for instance, to objectify their problem construction, to identify problem-saturated stories, and to connect, energize, and expand upon stories that bring forth their strengths. This focus on meaning rather than behavior allows clients to see alternative ways to engage reality. Pictures, stories, and metaphors are used in therapy to give clients a more inclusive view and meaning of life.

The social constructionist and RSM perspectives give primary attention to present but not yet manifest contextual governing forces. The socially constructed items we call values, beliefs, priorities, etc., are handed down to us by the specific context in which we live. To varying extents, we internalize these handed-down powerful "truths" and make them part of the language we use to engage life. In the sense that we adopt a context item, internalize it, and make it a part of our created-selves, each of us co-creates the items in our context.

As part of our language process we form life stories or narratives about our life. Critical to the therapeutic process is our conscious awareness that our life stories are written, directed, played out, and produced out of our own selves.

It is important that we truly know that our life story, like all stories, is incomplete. Out of many possible "themes" we select one that exclusively governs our life and is the receptacle for almost all of our awareness while we give other parts of our lives little or no attention. The overattached items push the other items into the background, but those unnoticed parts of our lives continue to exist and to exert a strong influence over us. To put it another way, we live in a sea of experiences. Each of us recognizes only parts of that vast sea. The parts we distinguish are in synchrony with the personal constructions that we have internalized and that have governing power over us.

Again, the key to dealing with context-reality is to give conscious attention to the labels, stories, and metaphors each of us claims as our own. Conscious attention to context items enables us to be aware of the constructed social forces that govern and move us through life. An important perspective for all people is one that reflectively asks what is not true and what is being left out in the nature of a particular context.

SPIRITUAL

The fourth reality, the spiritual, is our innate sense that as living, thinking, self-aware beings each of us is a part of a greater whole. Within each of us is the spark of life that comes from a creator and ruler of the universe.

> Here we are talking about a reality that presupposes the existence of a sentience (a state of awareness) beyond the human senses, a reality that is capable of acting outside of the observed principles and limitations of the natural sciences *and* a force that makes demands upon its adherents. This human sense of a transcendent authority, an ultimate context, has been found in all known human cultures. Surveys in our country have consistently found that over 90% of the people in the United States believe in God. (Bardill, 1997, p. 25)

The spiritual reality is subject to considerable misunderstanding. For instance, while the spiritual reality is expounded in the context of religion, religion is human made. Spiritual reality and religion are not the same. Religion is the human-made form of, and relationship to, the spiritual reality. The spiritual reality, when subjected to the forms of institutional religion, is part of the context-reality.

The general human yearning to connect to the spiritual reality, to

God, may lead people to fail to distinguish between that which is of God and that which is human made–the context reality. A simple distinguishing perspective may be useful here. If a created item is destructive to human life and well-being it cannot be an outworking of the spiritual.

From yet another perspective the individual human's yearning to connect with the spiritual reality may lead to a search within one's self for the "god within." There are many and various ways people seek to connect with the spiritual reality. For instance, in the Christian world view a person connects with God through a faith relationship to Jesus Christ. Other spiritual world views suggest different avenues for connecting to the spiritual. An effective therapist is aware that, for many people, the spiritual is an organizing force for all that they think, feel, and do. For these people the spiritual reality is indeed a powerful reality.

The universal concern about and attention to the spiritual realm over the history of humankind raises a fundamental question. The question is straightforward yet it addresses a divine mystery of life: Does God exist? Take a moment to reflect and think about your answer. When you have proposed an answer ask yourself two compelling follow-up questions.

If you answered, No, God does not exist, the necessary follow-up question that *must* be answered is: On what basis do I anchor myself in life? If there is no absolute context for life, what are the sources of guidance for human values and conduct? Left to my own devices where will I locate my moral being? All humans live from some philosophical base whether they are aware of it or not. The history of humankind tells us that without God humans must turn to themselves for a code of social conduct. The vehicle for the content and process of such a code of conduct becomes the laws of a society as carried out by its people of that society.

If your answer to the fundamental question about God's existence is Yes, there is a God, the follow-up question must be, What is the nature of God? To know that there is a God who is creator and ruler of the universe and not to seek God's nature is an existential contradiction.

A basic ethical and procedural value for psychotherapy is to begin where the client is. Beginning where the client is addresses the nature of the client's connection to all of the realities, including the spiritual reality. In that sense ethical and effective psychotheorists are deeply aware of the nature of their own connections to the spiritual reality. In the RSM ethical and effective psychotherapy is respectful and attentive to the spiritual.

SELF-DIFFERENTIATION

The treatment implications of RSM are likely to be enhanced through an integration of self-differentiation dynamics and the realities. A vital part of the human emotional process has been captured in the idea of self-differentiation. The relevance of the differentiation process to the human emotional system was first introduced by Murray Bowen (1978). Differentiation is a term primarily used in biology to address the separateness of interrelated parts to make up the whole human body. For Bowen the concept addresses the degree of fusion or differentiation between emotional and intellectual functioning (Bowen, 1978, p. 362). Ed Friedman regarded differentiation as the capacity to become one's self out of one's self with a minimum reactivity to the position of reactivity of others (Friedman, 1991).

Building on the work of Bowen and Friedman, RSM posits the self-differentiation process is the key to an individual's successful connections to the life realities. A well differentiated person enjoys self-management in three psychosocially defining processes–self-regulation, self-definition, and self-distinction.

SELF-REGULATION

The process of self-regulation deals with the degree of an individual's ability to distinguish among internal thinking, emotions, and survival energies, and to keep thinking energies and process in charge of one's life responses. Survival, emotions, and thinking energies are all necessary ingredients for full human functioning. Human relationship problems emerge when the emotions and survival functions govern our actions rather than support thinking functioning. The straightforward question is, What part of my brain functioning is in charge?

SELF-DEFINITION

We have two strong yearnings that are at the same time contradictory and complementary. As humans we want to be separate, autonomous persons who reach our full potential in life. We want to have time to ourselves, to have personal influence on life, and to enjoy a sense of personal value. We want to love others of our own free will. At the same time we have equally powerful yearnings to be together with other people, to enjoy close relationships with others, to be part of the scheme of life, and to sense that we are loved and cared for by others. The self-definition process works to maintain a balance between yearning to be separate and yearning to be together with others. Self-definition means that we know exactly who and what we are in close relationships to others, to the context, and to the spiritual. In other words we are fully connected to ourselves, others, the context, and the spiritual.

SELF-DISTINCTION

The process of self-distinction engages the innate human capacity to create such items as values, beliefs, ideas, identities, roles, priorities, pictures, images, language, stories, etc., for the purposes of survival, safety, and growth. The real-self is the creative capacity every human has to use their whole brain and nervous system to be fully functional. The self-distinction process also engages a human inclination to fuse with that which we create and thus blur the distinction between the creator and the created. When we come to regard a created life item as real-self, any threat to that created item energizes emotionalized survival reactions thereby increasing the possibility of dysfunctional behavior.

A well differentiated therapist will use the process of self-management to provide a treatment atmosphere that invites clients to examine that part of life they want to change. As for the therapist, it is rumored that Murray Bowen once said something to the effect that if you don't know what to do just be there with the client and self-differentiate. Indeed, clinical experiences shows that engaging the self-differentiation process moves the treatment forward.

CONCLUSION

The guiding theme of RSM is to bring forth that which is present but not yet manifest. Ideally, the therapy process is guided by a well-differentiated therapist who prompts the client–individual, couple, or family–to fully engage the realities of life. The secret of all successful therapy is to put in what is missing for the client, i.e., that part of self, other, context, and spiritual that is waiting to be brought forth.

REFERENCES

Andreas, S., & Satir, V. (1991). *The patterns of her magic*. Palo Alto, CA: Science and Behavior Books, Inc.

Bardill, D. R. (1997). *The relational systems model for family therapy: Living in the four realities*. Binghamton, NY: The Haworth Press, Inc.

Bardill, D. R. (1997). The spiritual reality: A Christian world view. In D. S. Becvar (Ed.), *The family, spirituality and social work*. Binghamton, NY: The Haworth Press, Inc.

Bowen, M. (1978). *Family therapy in clinical practice*. New York: Jason Aronson.

Connerae, A., & Andreas, S. (1989). *Heart of the mind*. Moab, UT: Real People Press.

Eron, J. B., & Lund, T. (1996). *Narrative solutions in brief therapy*, New York: Guilford Press.

Friedman, E. N. (1991). Bowen theory and therapy. In A. Gurman, & D. K. Kriskern (Eds.), *Handbook of family therapy*: Vol. 11. New York: Brunner/Mazel.

Hoffman, L. Constructing realities: An art of senses, *Family Process, 29*; 1-12, 1990.

Popper, K. R. (1965). *Conjectures and refutations*. London: Routledge and Kegan Paul.

Satir, V., Banman, J., Gerber, J., & Gomori, M. (1991). *The Satir model: Family therapy and beyond*. Palo Alto, CA: Science and Behavior Books, Inc.

White. M., & Epston, D. (1990). *Narrative means to therapeutic ends*. New York: W.W. Norton.

Towards an Understanding of Religious People's Perceptions and Lived Experiences of Religion and Spirituality: Implications for Marriage and Family Therapists

Charles J. Joanides, PhD
Harvey Joanning, PhD
Patricia Keoughan, PhD

SUMMARY. This paper presents the reader with a systematic description of religious people's perceptions of religion and spirituality. Results from 24 Lutheran and Greek Orthodox respondents suggest (a) that religion and spirituality profoundly impact the manner in which religious people view the world, (b) that religious people view religion as more than a human construction, (c) that religious people view religion and spirituality as interrelated and interconnected spheres of experience, and (d) that salient contextual information can be missed when therapists/researchers fail to address religion and spirituality from religious people's perspectives. Implications for MFTs, and MFT researchers, are also discussed. *[Article copies available for a fee from The Haworth Document Delivery Service: 1-800-342-9678. E-mail address: <getinfo@haworthpressinc.com> Website: <http://www.haworthpressinc.com>]*

Charles J. Joanides is Director, Interfaith Research Project for the Greek Orthodox Archdiocese of America. He also pastors St. Nicholas Greek Orthodox Church, Newburgh, NY. Harvey Joanning is Professor and Director, Marriage and Family Therapy Doctoral Program, Department of Human Development and Family Studies, Iowa State University, Ames, IA. Patricia Keoughan is President, Human Systems Consultants, Inc., Ames, IA and is Instructor, Counselor Education Program, Iowa State University, Ames, IA.

[Haworth co-indexing entry note]: "Towards an Understanding of Religious People's Perceptions and Lived Experiences of Religion and Spirituality: Implications for Marriage and Family Therapists." Joanides, Charles J., Harvey Joanning, and Patricia Keoughan. Co-published simultaneously in *Journal of Family Social Work* (The Haworth Press, Inc.) Vol. 4, No. 3, 2000, pp. 79-97; and: *Social Work and the Family Unit* (ed: David J. Ludwig) The Haworth Press, Inc., 2000, pp. 79-97. Single or multiple copies of this article are available for a fee from The Haworth Document Delivery Service [1-800-342-9678, 9:00 a.m. - 5:00 p.m. (EST). E-mail address: getinfo@haworthpressinc.com].

KEYWORDS. Religion, spirituality, client systems, religious development, church community, religious education, moral development, spiritual experiences, transformative experiences, synergy

Marriage and family therapists (MFTs) have recently shown an
interest in their clients' religious and spiritual experiences (Anderson
& Worthen, 1997; Becvar, 1994; Berenson, 1990; Butler, 1988; Friedman, 1985; Goldberg, 1994; Griffith, 1986; Joanides, 1996; Joanides,
1997; Prest & Keller, 1993; Ross, 1994; Stander, Piercy, Mackinnion
& Helmeke, 1994; Stewart & Gale, 1994; Weaver, Koenig & Larson,
1997). Despite the relative newness of this literature, many convincing
arguments have been generated that both encourage and justify the
inclusion of religious and spiritual concerns during therapy. As significant as these above efforts have been, some perceived deficiencies
may exist. Specifically, from this author's Greek Orthodox religious
and theological background the following possible blind spots have
been detected.

- Some MFTs have generally tended to refer to religion and spirituality as if these experiences are somehow connected to one
another. These clinicians have not, however, carefully examined
their interconnectedness and interdependence.
- Some MFTs writing about religion and spirituality appear to cir-
cumvent religious concerns, and prefer to focus most of their
attention on spiritual experiences that appear to be more global in
nature.
- Some MFTs appear to have focused attention on the topic of
religion from a multicultural perspective, and have tended to de-
emphasize an examination of the client system's spiritual experi-
ence(s).

These above approaches may be delimiting for the following reasons. Religious people may view religion as more than a cultural by
product and human construction. Religious people may also not perceive and experience religion and spirituality in dichotomous terms.
Religious people may experience and discern these two spheres of
experience as being both distinct and profoundly interrelated to one
another. As a way to investigate these concerns, therefore, the following two-part research question was utilized:

Are religious people's lived experiences and perceptions of
religion and spirituality inherently dichotomous or intercon-

nected in nature? If religious people do not dichotomize these two experiences, how do they perceive these experiences, and what are the ramifications for MFTs.

METHODOLOGY

About the Researcher and His Approach to This Research Project

Before proceeding further, the reader should be aware of certain collateral, but pertinent information about the researcher. Specifically, this researcher has been a Greek Orthodox priest for 18 years and views himself as a religious person whose religious orientation profoundly influences the manner in which he views the world. He believes that one's religious tradition has an exceedingly acute impact on one's spirituality and vice versa and maintains that there is a synergistic relationship that exists between religious people's religious and spiritual experiences. He does not, therefore, view or approach religion and spirituality as if these two phenomena are entirely unrelated spheres of experience, nor does he believe that religion and spirituality function independently of one another in religious people's lives. Furthermore, as an MFT, he believes that when therapists are disinterested in their religious clients' religiosity and spirituality, such an approach could negatively impact therapy with religious client systems. He has also embraced and utilizes a postmodern approach to research which assumes that all research is driven by theoretical presuppositions and assumptions (Doherty, Boss, Larossa, Schumm & Steinmetz, 1993; Suppe, 1977; Thomas & Roghaar, 1990). He further maintains that both religious and non-religious researchers should be conducting research in this area, with one important proviso, i.e., that researchers identify their religious or non-religious biases within the body of their text as will be done throughout this paper (McNamara, 1988).

A Qualitative Grounded Theory Approach

There are a number of methodological approaches available to qualitative researchers (Denzin & Lincoln, 1994). Each approach is uniquely suited to the research question being considered (Denzin & Lincoln, 1994). Since one of the objectives of this research was to generate a thick, rich, systematic description of religious people's perceptions of the terms religion and spirituality, a grounded theory approach was selected and utilized as the method of choice for this research project (Glaser & Strauss, 1967; Strauss & Corbin, 1990; 1994). As applied to this research, a grounded theory approach assisted the researcher in his efforts to generate a thick, rich systematic description that would be conceptually grounded in religious people's lived experiences.

Description of the Sampling Technique

In an effort to develop descriptions that were not based entirely on one religious group's observations and interpretations of the terms religion and spirituality, respondents were recruited from two separate Christian denominations. Specifically, since the researcher had direct access to Lutherans and Eastern Orthodox Christians, respondents for this study were selected from the Evangelical Lutheran Church of America (ECLA) and from the Greek Orthodox Church of America (GOA). It should also be noted here that this type of convenience sampling has proven to be sufficient when researchers seek to generate new ideas that are intended to lead to theory construction and theory verification (Strauss & Corbin, 1994; Sells, Smith & Sprenkle, 1995). This sampling approach also allows researchers the needed latitude to deliberately select respondents whom they judge will have relevance on a given research study (Lewis & Moon, 1997; Sells et al., 1995).

Description of Respondents

Respondents in this study were purposively selected on the basis of their ability to expound upon their religious and spiritual experiences (Strauss & Corbin, 1990). Twenty-four respondents participated in this study, i.e., with 12 of the 24 being from the ECLA, and twelve identifying themselves with the GOA. The reason why 24 respondents were included in this study was intimately linked to the information that was received toward the latter part of the data collection process. At or around the twentieth interview the researcher began receiving redundant information, and thus deemed that he had reached a saturation point: a point at which he was not gathering any substantially new information (Sells et al., 1995; Strauss & Corbin, 1990). The last four interviews were thus conducted to fill in certain blind spots, and assure the researcher that he had not failed to miss any salient components.

Twenty participants in this study reported that they were cradle Orthodox/Lutherans, while four stated that they were converts from other Christian denominations. Participants attended church weekly, and were moderately to highly active in their church community. Participants also considered themselves moderately to highly religious and spiritual persons. Participants' ages ranged from 35-67, with an average age of 43. Fourteen were females and ten were males. All participants in this study also had some college education. Nineteen participants reported being married with children, while five respondents stated being single. Participants resided in the following states: Colorado (3), Iowa (15), Massachusetts (4), and Minnesota (2).

Description of Interviewing Process and Techniques

The researcher sought to track the contents of each interview in an effort to discern respondents' level of comfort with the interview process and the extent to which respondents might be responding in a socially desirable manner. By proceeding in this manner, it was hoped that any latent, confounding affects that his role as interviewer and researcher would be reduced, and that respondents would be encouraged to assume a level of participation that allowed them to undertake the role of co-creators and co-constructors in this research.

Twenty-four 60-90 minute interviews were conducted. Since qualitative researchers do not find it necessary to transcribe each and every one of their interviews (Denzin & Lincoln, 1994; Strauss & Corbin, 1990), of the 24 interviews that were conducted, the researcher determined to transcribe every other interview. Additionally, after interviews were conducted and analyzed, eleven follow-up telephone interviews (lasting approximately 30 minutes) were conducted. During these follow-up interviews, the researcher sought to conduct member checks by reading his analysis to the respondent, and by soliciting comments and suggestions to assist him with any future interviews that would follow.

Types of Questions Utilized

Semi-structured sequential interviews were conducted with the contents of the questions changing as the interview process unfolded and new concerns and insights emerged. Close-ended questions were utilized to obtain some demographic information about each respondent. Semi-structured, open-ended questions were used to elicit as much information as possible from the respondents' perspectives without intentionally influencing their observations. The interview and analysis process was inherently incremental, iterative, and recursive in nature. Specifically, one ECLA participant and one GOA participant was separately interviewed. After each set of interviews was completed, debriefings (Joanides, Brigham & Joanning, 1997) were conducted with each participant, and an analysis of these interviews was conducted. Once the analysis process was completed, member checking occurred and, the semi-structured questionnaire was modified before the next set of interviews were conducted. The value of following this research protocol was as follows: (a) this process allowed the questions and answers to build and unfold incrementally, thereby avoiding any predetermined presuppositions on the part of the researcher from guiding this research (Sells et al., 1995; Strauss & Corbin, 1990), (b) this process allowed respondents to assume the role of teacher, co-researcher, and co-collaborator (Sells et al., 1995), and (c) this process allowed for the shared constructions of the respondents and researcher to co-evolve (Sells et al., 1995; Struass & Corbin, 1990).

Techniques Used to Ensure Trustworthiness

Code notes were used to assist the researcher in generating conceptual labels, categories, properties, and dimensions which would ultimately function to form the essential features of the thick rich descriptions proposed in this paper (Strauss & Corbin, 1990). Theoretical notes were employed to assist the researcher in his efforts to begin (a) conceptualizing and formulating relevant subcategories, their properties and dimensions, (b) assist him in discerning the given relationships that existed between the subcategories, properties, and dimensions, and (c) help him in his efforts to discover some of the essential features of the systematic description that would ultimately be generated through this effort (Strauss & Corbin, 1990). And finally, operational notes were comprised of memos that would provide the researcher with direction regarding sampling, questions, and the possible comparisons that he should follow up on as the research process continued (Strauss & Corbin, 1990).

In order to ensure that credibility, transferability, dependability and confirmability issues were considered and satisfied (Lincoln & Guba, 1985) the following techniques were also employed. The use of member checks, peer debriefing, persistent observation and the establishment of referential adequacy served to ensure that credibility issues were considered (Lincoln & Guba, 1985). The use of purposive sampling and the researcher's efforts to generate a thick, rich, systematic description of respondent's perceptions would serve to satisfy transferability issues (Lincoln & Guba, 1985). The use of an audit trail would serve to meet dependability issues (Lincoln & Guba, 1985). The use of an external auditor and the researcher's efforts to practice reflexivity would serve to meet confirmability issues (Lincoln & Guba, 1985).

Coding Procedures and Techniques Utilized

Analysis proceeded in three stages (Strauss & Corbin, 1990). In the first stage, typically termed "open coding," the researcher attempted to open the data up in an effort to begin building a conceptual framework. This process also (a) allowed the researcher to tentatively begin grouping concepts together and collapsing them under cover terms that are called categories and subcategories, (b) assisted him in tentatively identifying different attributes and characteristics (properties) of each category called properties, and (c) allowed him to begin dimensionalizing each given property. The second stage in the analysis process, termed "axial coding" (Strauss & Corbin, 1990), allowed the researcher to piece together the data that had been taken apart during the first stage of analysis. Axial coding also served to assist the researcher in his efforts to begin putting his respondent's descriptions and interpretations of their religious and spiritual lived experiences back together in a systematic form. The third stage in this analysis process is termed "selective coding" (Strauss & Corbin, 1990). During this stage the researcher typically sought to explicate and identify a story line that was conceptually and systematically dense, and was derived from the collected data.

ANALYSIS

An analysis of respondent's observations and interpretations of the terms religion and spirituality generated the following main category: religious people's religious and spiritual lived experiences are distinctly separate, yet inherently synergistic and interrelated in character. The following four subcategories were also generated: (a) religiosity and spirituality are developmental in character, (b) lived religious experiences, (c) lived spiritual experiences, and (d) religion and spiritual: their interconnectedness. In addition, a collateral subcategory also emerged entitled: implications for marriage and family therapists. Twenty-seven interrelated properties or attributes of the four subcategories also surfaced, as well as 167 interrelated dimensions or attributes of the 27 properties.

Subcategory #1: The Developmental Character of Religiosity and Spirituality

Property #1 and dimensions: nature of religious development. All (24) respondents in this study repeatedly stated that religious people's religious and spiritual experiences are not static in character, but are instead distinctly dynamic and developmental in character.

Property #2 and dimensions: baptism. All respondents (24) in this study viewed baptism as an important life experience that served to mark the beginning of their religious and spiritual development. All respondents (24) in this study tended to state that baptism was instituted by Jesus Christ, inspired by God, performed within a corporate church setting, and was essentially a personal experience. Most respondents (20) also indicated that baptism functions to connect the baptized person to something greater than the self, i.e., the church community, one's neighbors, God, or all three. All respondents (24) stated that this ritual was the direct result of God's love, and people's desire to connect with "the Creator."

Property #3 and dimensions: significant others. All respondents (24) in this study also indicated that significant others were intimately involved in their religious and spiritual development, i.e., such as parents, grandparents, clergy, Sunday school teachers, and religious counselors.

Property #4 and dimensions: death and tragedy. Many respondents (13) also indicated that "the death of a loved one" had contributed to their religious and spiritual development. Others (14) talked about how knowledge of their own mortality had impacted their religious and spiritual development. In this latter case, respondents who were 50 or older were more inclined to consider their own "mortality" and how the passing of time has increased their religious participation and development.

Property #5 and dimensions: church community. All (24) participants in this study also consistently referred to the primary importance that their church community had (and continued to have) on their religious and spiritual development. Religious community support was judged to be (a) helpful to one's formative and adolescent development, (b) was nurturing and comforting during times of crisis, and (c) provided one with a kind of prefabricated social network. All respondents (24) also alluded to the value of corporate worship and the "liturgical" and "sacramental life" of their respective faith communities. They generally tended to believe that corporate prayer life provided them with a "framework" that enhanced their religious and spiritual development. Others (13) also stated that their efforts to develop a deeper more personal understanding of their church's corporate worship positively affected the manner in which they have come to discern and value religion and spirituality.

Property #6 and dimensions: religious education. Catechetical training of the type that one received in Sunday school was also mentioned as an important component in all (24) respondents' efforts to develop a religious and spiritual life. Respondents (17) stated that Bible Stories, and stories about faithful historical figures from church history ("the saints") were immensely helpful in their formative years. Respondents (15) also indicated that their participation in philanthropic endeavors, fellowship groups, and adult religious education classes have served to positively impact their religious and spiritual development.

Property #7 and dimensions: time and commitment. All respondents (24) pointed to the significance of offering a specific time commitment to a religious community. Respondents tended to highlight the positive impact that "meaningful participation," "discipline," "consistency," and "regular commitment" in a religious community can have on a person's religious and spiritual development.

Property #8 and dimensions: God's grace. All respondents (24) also repeatedly mentioned "God's grace" as being pivotal in their religious development. Some (13) utilized the descriptors, "Divine energy," some (11) used "Divine love" and several (5) used "God's light" or "God's life" to emphasize the central importance God's role in their efforts to become religious and spiritual.

Property #9 and dimensions: cohort effects. Respondents (12) also referred to certain cohort/historical events that they felt had made profound impacts on their religious and spiritual development such as "The Great Depression," "World War II," and "The Sixties."

Property #10 and dimensions: negative religious experiences. Respondents (15) also referred to a number of negative religious experiences that had initially impacted their religious and spiritual development in adverse ways. These respondents stated that Divine consolation and guidance had either assisted them in changing their perception of these negative experiences, or helped them reduce the negative affects.

Subcategory #2: Lived Religious Experiences

Property #1 and dimensions: corporate/social character of religion. All (24) respondents described religion as a corporate experience. Many respondents (17) also alluded to religion as a "social institution" and "organized activity." Additionally, when these participants attempted to describe their experiences in more detailed terms, they tended to refer to a corporate experience that was at once held together by common beliefs, common rituals, common history, and common goals and objectives.

Property #2 and dimensions: framework and structure. All respondents (24) viewed religion as providing them with the "framework" or "structure" that facilitated their personal efforts to "draw closer to the Transcendent." All (24) respondents also tended to refer to a collection of distinct, yet interdependent religious "forms" that were essential components of what they perceived as their religious framework or structure, i.e., such as icons, the Bible, candles, etc. All (24) respondents also stated that these "forms" served to assist religious people in their efforts to communicate with the Divine.

Property #3 and dimensions: perceived origins of religion. All (24) respondents viewed religion as a human experience that was Divinely inspired and has co-evolved through a process of human cooperation and Divine inspiration. In these instances, respondents appeared to insist that religious activity was less a result of a social convention, and more the result of a "God-given" inherent drive.

Property #4 and dimensions: moral development. All respondents (24) in this study also agreed that religion was "absolutely crucial" and "central" to religious people's moral and ethical development. All respondents (24) also indicated that either all or part of the "rules and regulations" had been inspired by God, and as such, were generally viewed in absolute terms vis-à-vis relative terms. Most (18) respondents also viewed these moral guidelines as "transformative" in character. These respondents tended to believe that these moral guidelines possessed the ability to impact the manner in which religious people view life, struggle with problems, attempt to communicate with God's goodness, and assist them to value others.

Property #5 and dimensions: impact on respondent's world view. All respondents (24) in this study also judged that their religious orientation profoundly impacted the manner in which they viewed both the world and their neighbor. As such, all (24) respondents repeatedly used terms such as "a world view," "a lens," and a "lifestyle" to refer to religion.

Property #6 and dimensions: personal stability, meaning and security. All respondents (24) suggested that religion provided them with "a sense of meaning," and "answers" to seemingly unanswerable questions or troublesome topics such as "death," "tragedy," and "sickness." Many (15) spoke repeatedly of religion's ability to provide the believer with a sense of security in an unpredictable, precarious existence. Many respondents (16) also alluded to religion's uncanny ability (a) to link them with the past, and (b) the consolation that such a connection offered them.

Property #7 and dimensions: political nature of religion. Some respondents (11) also alluded to the political nature of religion. In these instances, these respondents essentially viewed the political nature of religion as potentially "pathological," and as "destructive behavior" which was more the result of humankind's proclivity to misunderstand and misinterpret the quintessential purpose of religion.

Property #8 and dimensions: enhancing dialogue with the Divine. All (24) respondents generally agreed that religion enhances religious people's dialogue with the Divine, and assists religious people in their efforts to connect with God.

Subcategory #3: Lived Spiritual Experiences

All (24) respondents clearly and repeatedly (a) believed in a Transcendent Being, (b) believed that the Divine makes "Himself" accessible to humankind in a personal way, (c) alluded to certain explicit "spiritual exercises" and devotional processes that were routinely performed to facilitate a relationship with the Divine, and (d) described a synergistic process between the individual and God, whose ultimate effects were transformative in character or served to profoundly impact each respondent's perception of themselves, their neighbor and the world around them.

Property #1 and dimensions: a personal, esoteric connection with God. All (24) respondents initially stated that their perception of the term spirituality was founded on an "internal mystical experience" or "internal connection" with the Divine. Moreover, when respondents were asked to elaborate upon these statements, all (24) remarked that this connection with the Divine was more of a "personal search" which led to a "personal" experience with God, as compared to their religious lived experiences which were essentially framed within a corporate/social experience.

Property #2 and dimensions: a relationship with the Divine. Respondents (24) in this study also compared their spiritual connection to God with "a relationship" and generally tended to utilize this metaphor to describe their spirituality. Most (19) also referred to a prayerful dialogue that they engaged in with God that they compared with the "communication" that takes place within "other more familiar types" of relationships.

Property #3 and dimensions: a transformative experience. All (24) respondents also stated that this spiritual experience was "pervasive" and "transformative" in nature: meaning that their experience of the Divine tended to profoundly impact the manner in which these respondent's "viewed themselves," "their neighbor," and "all of creation." Specifically, they stated that their spiritual experiences with the Divine had (a) functioned to increase their awareness of life around them from "a self-centered perspective" to a more "holistic perspective," (b) strengthened their connection with their neighbor and assisted them in discerning how a relationship with neighbor is crucial to assisting them "in becoming all that they were created to be," and (c) sensitized and broadened their perception "of the holiness of all of creation" and their respective place in the universe.

Property #4 and dimensions: one's personal role in this process. All respondents (24) also described the part they personally felt they assumed within this process. Remarks made to describe the role that these respondents perceived they owned in this relationship included descriptors such as "personal discipline," "faith," "daily devotions," "practicing prayer," "continual response," "persistence," "priorities," etc.

Subcategory #4: Religion and Spirituality: Their Interconnectedness

Properties #1/#2 and dimensions: differences in religion and spirituality. All (24) respondents in this study viewed religion and spirituality as two distinct experiences. Concurrently, all (24) respondents consistently emphasized that they did not think of these experiences in dichotomous terms.

Property #3 and dimensions: interconnectedness/interdependence. All (24) participants in this study perceived religion and spirituality as two experiences that are intrinsically "interconnected" and "interdependent" with one another.

Properties #4/#5 and dimensions: a synergy/dialectic. All (24) respondents in this study agreed that religion and spirituality "work together" and are "interrelated." Observations and descriptions such as "they go hand in hand," "there is a distinction, but there is also an overlap," "they are intertwined," and "there is a dialectic between these experiences," were repeatedly utilized to assist these respondents in their efforts to describe and conceptualize the manner in which these terms are both viewed and experienced.

Property #7 and dimensions: similarities between religion and spirituality. When given the opportunity to discuss the similarities between these two experiences all (24) respondents maintained that these two experiences were more alike than dissimilar. For example, when asked to describe the extent that these two experiences were similar, one respondent stated: "I would say 80-90 percent."

Subcategory #5: Implications for Psychotherapists

All (24) respondents felt that the inclusion of religious and spiritual concerns in the therapeutic process was essential. All (24) respondents stated that they would look for a therapist who was favorably inclined to including and respecting religious and spiritual concerns. Some (9) respondents also suggested that a religiously oriented therapist might be better suited to meeting their therapeutic needs for the following reasons. They speculated that there might be a better fit between themselves and a religious therapist who was familiar with their background. In these instances respondents essentially felt that (a) the quality of therapy would be positively impacted by a therapist with a similar religious and spiritual perspective and (b) that a religiously oriented therapist might be more inclined to include "Divine intercession," "Divine wisdom" and "Divine grace" into the therapeutic process.

Many (15) were not as concerned with their therapist's religious orientations, as they were with his/her respect for a client system's religiosity and spirituality. Moreover, some (5) respondents even suggested that they were leery of therapists who identified themselves as "Christian Counselors." Respondents who desired that their therapist include religious and spiritual concerns into the therapeutic process offered the following additional observations. First, all (24) respondents felt that the inclusion of religious and spiritual concerns (where applicable) into the therapeutic process would assist therapists in their efforts to comprehend a client's worldview. Second, many (13) respondents in this study also theorized that if therapists included religious and spiritual concerns into therapy with religious client systems, then these types of therapists would also likely be more capable of assisting religious people in their efforts to reconnect with family and society. Third, most (17) respondents in this study also felt as if they might be "more respected" by therapists who chose to include religious and spiritual concerns into the therapeutic process. These respondents tended to firmly believe that religion and spirituality functioned to profoundly influence who they were as people. As such, if their religiosity and spirituality were disregarded they imagined that they might feel "disrespected." Fourth, some (12) respondents in this study also supposed that therapists who were inclined to include religious and spiritual concerns during therapy might (a) facilitate the joining process with religious clients, and (b) acquire more confidence in their therapist as a result of his/her receptivity to this dimension of their lives.

Fifth, respondents (11) also felt that therapists who failed to include religious and spiritual concerns into therapy "might miss some great opportunity for counseling." Sixth, some (9) also supposed that a therapist's curiosity in how religion and spirituality impact a given client's distress might serve to "enrich" his/her questions. Seventh, others (16) also postulated that therapists who were interested in religion and spirituality might inadvertently assist religious persons in their efforts to utilize all their available resources during a particularly stressful time. Eighth, many (14) also pointed out that therapists working with individuals, marriages, and families might assist their clients in their efforts to resolve systemic conflict. Ninth, some (11) respondents also stated that the inclusion of religious and spiritual concerns might also function to enrich therapy by including a dimension of many people's lived experiences that is often ignored. Finally, all (24) respondents in this study stated that therapy that did not include a religious client's religiosity and spirituality would likely be tantamount to "bad therapy" for all the reasons mentioned above.

DISCUSSION AND CONCLUSIONS

Implications for MFTs

When considering how this research may inform the work that MFTs do with religious individuals and client systems, the following observations are offered to the reader for consideration.

First, MFTs have recently become increasingly sensitive to how gender, ethnicity, race, and other ecological and idiosyncratic variables influence human development and family relations. Similarly, results from this study strongly suggest that religion and spirituality appear to profoundly impact religious individuals and family systems. It is thus maintained that an investigation of the manner in which religion and spirituality affects religious people might prove to be beneficial to the psychotherapeutic process. It is also asserted that therapists who are receptive to including religious and spiritual concerns (where applicable) into the therapeutic process will likely develop a deeper, more sophisticated understanding of the world view of a religious client.

Second, an analysis of results also suggested that the inclusion of religion and spiritual concerns in therapy might function to facilitate the joining process with religious clients. When therapists utilize and incorporate a client system's language, opinions and world views into therapy, this strategy serves to facilitate a healthy working relationship between therapists and the client system whose ultimate affects serve to enhance the quality of therapy and, by extension, make the process more efficient and cost effective.

Third, results also suggest that religious people appear to select therapists who are respectful of religious people's religious perspectives, and are favorably disposed to including religious and spiritual concerns into therapy. Moreover, results also indicated that some religious people may believe that non-religious oriented therapists may be disrespectful to religious people's theistic view of the world. It is thus recommended that therapists should consider evaluating their personal level of religious sensitivity and how they evaluate their client's level of religiosity and spirituality. It is further posited that therapists failing to assess their client's religiosity and spirituality may inadvertently be metacommunicating disrespect for religious clients' religious/theistic perspectives. Conversely, results also suggest that therapists who identify themselves as "Christian counselors" (or with some other similar identifier) may be perceived by some religious people with some suspicion. To be more specific, results from this study appear to suggest that some religious people may view "Christian counselors" as possessing a narrow, myopic therapeutic lens, i.e., one which some religious people may discern as limited in scope and less effective. Therapists who have determined to specialize their efforts, and focus their work on religious populations, might spend time during intake sessions addressing religious client systems' concerns about their expertise and approach.

Fourth, therapists choosing to include religious and spiritual concerns in therapy with religious client systems might also discover that this approach might assist religious people in their efforts to reconnect with family and other social systems. Specifically, results from this study appear to suggest religious and spiritual experiences facilitate and promote an interconnectedness between religious people and their social environment, and that religion and spirituality are two potentially powerful resources that could assist religious people in their efforts to repair interpersonal conflict.

Fifth, results from this study appear to indicate that therapists who work with self-described religious clients and families should consider religion and spirituality holistically rather than dichotomizing these two spheres of experience. Specifically, such an approach would tend to emphasize the systemic and recursive nature between these two related experiences, and the impact that both experiences have on a given religious client's or family's lived experience. Such an approach would also tend to enrich the therapeutic conversation, and allow for the emergence of a more accurate picture of a religious client system's lived experience. And finally, therapists adopting a more integrative or holistic view of religion and spirituality vis-à-vis a reductionistic approach, might also be less inclined to misdiagnose and pathologize certain religious behavior and behavioral patterns.

Implications for MFT Researchers

Participants' observations suggest that religious people may tend to embrace theistic paradigms to assist them in observing and interpreting the world, as compared to social scientists, who tend to utilize atheistic based paradigms that have been largely influenced by natural, evolutionary, positivistic, modernistic assertions (Thomas & Marsh, 1995; Vandenberg, 1992). In consequence, it is maintained that these differences may have compelled previous generations of social scientists (who were influenced by modernistic and positivistic paradigms) to both ignore and misinterpret religious and spiritual phenomena (Thomas & Marsh, 1995; Vandenberg, 1992). It is further argued that postmodern, postpositivistic approaches that view knowledge and theory as being largely consensual, context bound and self referential may be key to assisting social scientists in their efforts to examine certain human experiences that have heretofore been considered outside of the traditional paradigmatic purview of human science, religion and spirituality being indicative of two spheres of human experience that have essentially been ignored.

This research also suggested that a thorough understanding of religious phenomena may stand outside of the boundaries of scientific research simply because of social sciences' inability to verify certain sacred experiences, such as God's existence and religious people's belief in a Transcendent Being. Participants' descriptions of their religious experiences appeared to be embodied within a mystical experience with a Transcendent Being: one that profoundly impacted that manner in which respondents in this study observed and interpreted themselves, their neighbor, the world around them, and their ancestral past.

This research also served to suggest that religious people appear to experience religion and spirituality in more holistic terms. Research methodologies attempting to investigate religion and spirituality that are innately reductionistic in character may (on their own) be inadvertently disrespectful and wholly inadequate approaches. More qualitative and qualitative/quantitatiive research studies are thus needed if MFTs hope to develop a broader conceptual understanding of religious people's world view.

Results also pointed to the developmental character of these religious people's experiences of religion and spirituality, and suggested that researchers must be cognizant of their respondents' age, level of religiosity, and cohort affects. Research that is not reflective of the developmental character of religion and spirituality is likely to produce incomplete and skewed results. To that end, MFT researchers investigating religion and spirituality may consider whether religion and spirituality are perceived and utilized differently by the elderly than by people who are located at other earlier nodal stages in the life cycle. Results also suggested that researchers utilizing assessment tools should ensure that their instruments account for the multifaceted and developmental nature of the terms religion and spirituality.

Suggestions for Future Research

Further qualiative and qualitative/quantitative research is needed to determine if the observations offered in this study hold true for other religious denominations or faith traditions. Juxtaposing religious people with nominally religious people in a similar qualitative study may also prove invaluable to social scientists' and psychotherapists' efforts to understand the role that religion and spirituality play in religious people's lives. In a similar manner, investigating a clinical sample of religious people's perceptions may also provide useful insights for MFTs who choose to include religious and spiritual concerns into the therapeutic process. And finally, as MFTs develop a more sophisticated understanding of the role that religion and spirituality play in religious people's lives, this effort will likely provide a stronger theoretical undergirding for the work that they do with religious people, and lead toward a more effectual delivery of their services.

REFERENCES

Anderson, D. A., & Worthen, D. (1997). Exploring a fourth dimension: Spirituality as a source for the couple therapist. *Journal of Marital and Family Therapy, 23*, 3-12.

Becvar, D. S. (1994, June). Can spiritual yearnings and therapeutic goals be melded? *Family Therapy News*, pp. 13-14.

Bererson, D. (1990). A systemic view of spirituality: God and twelve step programs as resources in Family Therapy. *Journal of Strategic and Systemic Therapies, 9*, 59-70.

Butler, K. (1988). Spirituality reconsidered. *Family Therapy Networker, 14*, 26-37.

Denzin, N. K., & Lincoln, Y. S. (1994). *Handbook of Qualitative Research*. Thousand Oaks, CA: Sage.

Doherty, W. J., Boss, P. G., LaRossa, R., Schumm, W. R., & Steinmetz, S. K. (1993). Family theories and methods: A contextual approach. In P. G. Boss, W. J. Doherty, R. LaRossa, W. R. Schumm, S. K. Steinmetz (Eds.), *Sourcebook of family theories and methods: A contextual approach* (pp. 3-30). New York: Plenum Press.

Friedman, E. (1985). *Generation to Generation: Family Process in Church and Synagogue*. New York: Guilford.

Glaser, B. G., & Strauss, A. L. (1967). *The discovery of grounded theory: Strategies for qualitative research*. New York: Aldine.

Griffith, J. L. (1986). Employing the God-family relationship with religious families. *Family Process, 25*, 609-618.

Joanides, C. (1996). Collaborative family therapy with religious family systems. *Journal of Family Psychotherapy, 7*, 19-35.

Joanides, C. J. (1997). A qualitative investigation of the meaning of religion and spirituality to a group of Orthodox Christians: Implications for marriage and family therapists. *Journal of Family Social Work, 2*, 59-76.

Joanides, C. J., Brigham, L., & Joanning, H. (1997). Co-creating a more cooperative client-therapist relationship through a debriefing process. *The American Journal of Family Therapy, 25.*

Kosimin, B. A., & Lachman, S. P. (1995). Religious self-identification. In K. B. Bedell (Ed.). *Yearbook of American and Canadian Churches 1995.* New York: Abingdon Press.

Lewis, K. G., & Moon, S. (1997). Always single and single again women: A qualitative study. *Journal of Marital and Family Therapy, 23,* 115-134.

Lincoln, Y., & Guba, E. (1985). *Naturalistic Inquiry,* Beverly Hills, CA: Sage.

McNamara, P. H. (1988). The new Christian right's view of the family and its social science critics: A study in differing presuppositions. In D. L. Thomas (Ed.), *The religion and family connection: Social science perspectives.* Provo, UT: Religious Studies Center, Brigham Young University.

Prest, L. A., & Keller, J. F. (1993). Spirituality and family therapy: Spiritual beliefs, myths and metaphors. *Journal of Marital and Family Therapy, 19,* 137-148.

Ross, J. L. (1994). Working with patients within their religious contexts: Religion, spirituality, and the secular therapist. *Journal of Systemic Therapies, 13,* 7-15.

Sells, S. P., Smith, T. E., & Sprenkle, D. H. (1995). Integrating qualitative and quantitative research methods: A research model. *Family Process, 34,* 199-218.

Stander, V., Piercy, F. P., Mackinnon, D., & Helmeke, K. (1994). Spirituality, religion and family therapy: Competing or complementary worlds? *The American Journal of Family Therapy, 22,* 27-41.

Stewart, S. P., & Gale, J. E. (1994). On hallowed ground: Marital therapy with couples on the religious right. *Journal of Systemic Therapies, 13,* 16-25.

Strauss, A., & Corbin, J. (1990). *Basics of qualitative research: Grounded theory procedures and techniques.* Newbury Park, CA: Sage.

Strauss, A., & Corbin, J. (1994). Grounded theory methodology: An overview. In N. K. Denzin & Y. S. Lincoln, (Eds.), *Handbook of Qualitative Research* (pp. 273-285). Thousand Oaks, CA: Sage.

Suppe, F. (1977). *The structure of scientific theories* (2nd edition). Urbana, IL: University of Illinois Press.

Thomas, D. L., & Marsh, D. B. (1995, November). *Towards a theory of the moral family: The antinomic transcendent family connection. Paper presented at the annual National Council of Family Relations Theory Construction and Research Methodology Workshop,* Portland, Oregon.

Thomas, D. L., & Roghaar, H. B. (1990). Postpositivist theorizing: A case of religion and the family. In J. Sprey (Ed.), *Fashioning family theory: New approaches.* Newbury Park, CA: Sage Publications.

Vandenberg, B. (1992). Sacred text, secular history and human development. *Family Perspective, 26,* 405-421.

Weaver, A. J., Koenig, H. G., & Larson, D. B. (1997). Marriage and family therapists and the clergy: A need for clinical collaboration, training, and research. *Journal of Marital and Family Therapy, 23,* 13-25.

Index

Active parenting, 37-49
Affirmation, as individual, 58-60
Age, and reasoning style, 40
Authoritative parenting, 37-49
Authority, outside, 42-44

BASE/PLACE dynamic, 51-63
Bethany Lutheran Church (Austin, TX), 51-63
Beyond the Best Interest of the Child (Goldstein), 32
Blaming, 2,4-7
Blended family, 19-20,31-35
Boundaries, 31-35,44-46

Communication, 47-48
Counseling Services of Catawba County (MC), 31-35

Discipline styles, 37-49
Double messages, 23

Empowerment, 24-25

Family, as PLACE and BASE, 51-63
Family dialogue, 46-49
Family history, 60-61
Family life stages, 51-63
Family relationships, as central to therapy, 1-30
Family routines, 47
Family time, 46-47
Family unit, as PLACE and BASE, 51-63

Florida State University, 65-77
Forgiveness, 34

Greek Orthodox Archdiocese of America, 79-97
Growing up, 27-29

Impulse-control disorder, 25-26
Individual affirmation, 58-60
Individual differences, of children, 39-44
Iowa State University, 79-97

Lenoir-Rhyne College (Hickory, NC), 1-30
Limits, 44-46
Love, unconditional, 51-63

Marital bond. *See* "WE"
Mind-spirit-body triad, 21-23

Outside authority, 42-44
Overcontrol disorder, 25

Painter/Pointer dynamic, 7-19
Parenting
    active, 37-49
    united front in, 3-4,37-49
Personal distress, as relationship problem, 20-21
Physical safety, 56
PLACE/BASE, family as, 51-63